D0119233

KNOW YOUR CAT

KNOW YOUR CAT

AN OWNER'S GUIDE TO CAT BEHAVIOR

BRUCE FOGLE, D.V.M.

Photography by Jane Burton

DORLING KINDERSLEY, INC.
NEW YORK

A DORLING KINDERSLEY BOOK

Project Editor Liza Bruml
Art Editor Clair Watson
Production Controller Hilary Stephens
Managing Editor Carolyn King
Managing Art Editor Nick Harris

First American Edition, 1991
10 9 8 7 6 5 4 3 2
Dorling Kindersley, Inc.,
232 Madison Avenue, New York,
N.Y. 10016

ISBN 1-879431-04-1
Library of Congress Catalog Card Number 91-060145

Originated by Colourscan, Singapore
Printed and bound in Italy by Arnoldo Mondadori, Verona.

CONTENTS

Do we really know cats?

Cats are absolutely magnificent. They control their emotions far better than we do. They are more agile than dogs or any other domestic animal. They are self-sufficient, self-possessed, independent, strong, quiet and exceptionally well built, with parts that wear out only with old age. However, we frequently misunderstand them and we do so because, unlike dogs, cats are in many ways quite different from us.

Seeking security
Although magnificent predators, cats are prey to many larger animals and hiding is a natural behavior.

Dogs, like humans, are pack animals. Both have developed a reliance upon and enjoyment of the companionship of their own kind. In the process of doing so, a dynamic range of welcoming or "come closer" body language has evolved: we smile and wave; dogs look alert, drop their ears back and wag their tails. But cats come from a different beginning. They evolved or, to be more accurate, are in the process of evolving from solitary hunters to a more sociable species. They moved into human society later than any other domesticated animal but suddenly, in this century, have become extremely popular pets. In the United States, there are more

Body language
With arched back and erect fur, this kitten is sending out a "go away" signal.

Making friends
This cat was handled when a young kitten, so she now enjoys being stroked by her owner.

Stimulating play
Playing with objects improves the young cat's mental and physical dexterity.

than 50 million cats; they are already more popular than dogs. Add the estimated 30 million in Russia, 50 million in the rest of Europe and countless other millions in Africa, Australia, Asia, the rest of the Americas and on various islands worldwide, and there are over 200 million domestic cats – the most successful feline that has ever existed.

Naturally tidy
This cat willingly uses his litter box – cleanliness is second nature to the cat.

Domestic cats are divided into two main groups: domestic pet cats and feral cats. Domestic pet cats live with human company. Usually raised by us, they are content to live in our homes and share our food and affection. In fact, for cats, humans often make better companions than other cats.

Keeping warm
Using well-developed heat receptors on their noses, these newborn kittens seek out each other for warmth.

Feral cats are domestic cats born in the wild and raised outside human communities. The only difference between ferals and pet cats is in their early upbringing. If they are denied human contact during the important first seven weeks of life, they will always retain a timid fear of us. Early contact with humans is vital.

Mothering instinct
The mother cat provides her kittens with warmth and food. The father has no role in their care.

Playing games
To begin with, the kittens in a litter play happily together. Eventually the games deteriorate into more serious squabbles.

Playful behavior
Provided with lifelong security, these kittens will still play together as adults.

The North African wild cat, from which our pets evolved, was a hunter. Even today, domestic cats retain a strong urge to hunt. However, when the North African cats chose to move into human communities – and it was their choice – they changed from solitary hunters to beggars. In the wild kittens will stop playing with each other when the need to hunt for food, protect themselves, mark out territories and find mates become dominant factors. Pet cats, with all their daily needs taken care of, often remain playful when mature, as they never have to grow up.

New pedigrees
These Tonkinese kittens are very affectionate. The breed is a relatively new one.

More new breeds of cat are being created now than ever before. Each new breed has obvious physical attributes such as the length and color of the coat, but there are additional differences in their behavior. Some cats are noisier than others, less clean, or friendlier with other household pets. Behavior also varies with age.

Comfy position
Curled up, this pet cat relaxes, knowing that his owner will provide all the necessary food and warmth.

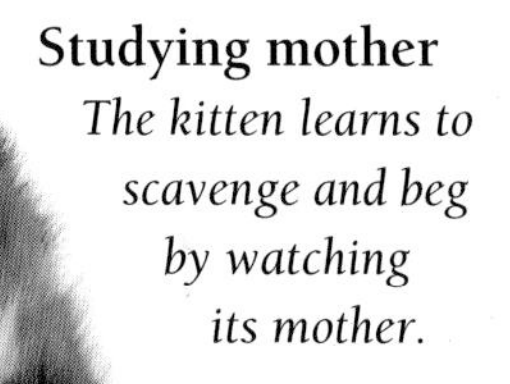

Studying mother
The kitten learns to scavenge and beg by watching its mother.

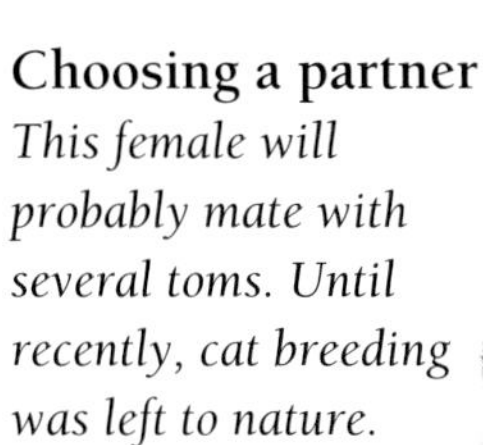

Choosing a partner
This female will probably mate with several toms. Until recently, cat breeding was left to nature.

Do cats really think? Of course they do. After all, look at your cat's reaction when it sees you get out the cat carrier for a visit to the veterinarian. Do cats have emotions? The answer is yes. And it is not anthropomorphic to credit cats with emotions such as jealousy, for both humans and cats have identical regions in the brain responsible for emotion. Through the book I am going to take this point one step further and put thoughts into the cat's mind. I am doing this to emphasize that they do have feelings and emotions, although I am aware that I may not always be reading their minds correctly.

Slowing down
In old age the cat's reaction time is reduced, but with improved health care and diet cats are living longer than ever.

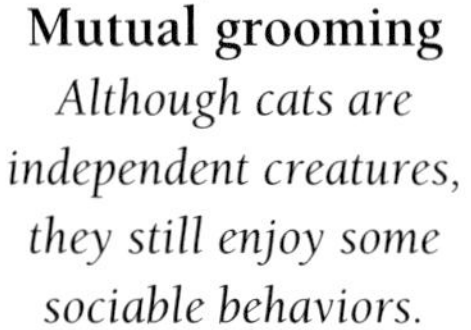

Mutual grooming
Although cats are independent creatures, they still enjoy some sociable behaviors.

Every day, on the examining table at my animal hospital, cats are telling me something. In most instances, it would probably not be suitable for publication, but my point is that through their body language and demeanor cats are skilled communicators. I hope I am acting as a good interpreter for them.

Quiet temperament
Flat-faced breeds are often calmer and more retiring than lithe oriental cats.

Reading faces
A relaxed expression can communicate happiness, contentment or curiosity.

Understanding Your Pet

Voicing complaints
A demand meow and an erect tail emphasize the urgency of this kitten's request.

CATS HAVE A magnificent variety of ways of communicating with each other. Some of their methods are so subtle that we human beings are not sensitive enough to understand what they are saying. Their use of body language is most often quiet, controlled and dignified. A mere flick of the tail, the slightest movement of the ears, the mildest dilation of the pupils – these messages are worth a thousand words to another cat. Because their body language is so restrained, and because we find it so difficult to understand, we make mistakes interpreting it.

The curious consequence of misunderstanding on our part is that we sometimes think that cats are deceitful. We believe they are lying to us with their bodies. In fact, they are telling us what they *really*

Threatening signals
Issuing a forceful hiss and staring with dilated pupils, this cat folds his ears back for protection.

Patrolling territory
With concentrated expression and alert ears, the cat patrols his territory daily, leaving visual and odor signals.

think, but in such subtle ways that we often fail to understand. It is easier for us to comprehend what cats are saying when they use their voices. Here, too, the range of sounds, from the purr to the happy "chirp," and the variety of meows, hisses, shrieks and spits, is gloriously extensive. Learning to make sense of the feline vocal range is a vital part of successful communication between cats and humans.

Cats indicate their territories with visual signs or with scent. Using their waste products as well as the scent-producing glands located on different parts of the skin, cats mark out humans and their environment. Unburied droppings or scratched fence posts and tree trunks silently communicate ownership of territory. Yards are perfect places to leave both scent and visual signals to neighborhood cats.

Increasing bulk
By arching his back, standing sideways and stiffening his body fur, this cat is trying to appear larger than he actually is.

Telling tails
A flicking tail usually indicates ambivalence, but also developing anger or annoyance.

Interpreting Cat Personality

ALTHOUGH ALL CATS share some behavior patterns with all other cats, each individual has its own personality. Some are friendly, assertive and bold; others are nervous, timid and shy. Personality differences originate in the genes – female blue-eyed white cats, for example, are likely to be timid. But early experience at kitten stage is also very important in creating personalities. Kittens that are stroked and played with are more likely to develop into confident cats.

Definitions applied to human personalities can also be used to describe your cat. The extrovert or outgoing cat is sociable, lively, assertive and adventurous; the neurotic or reserved type is shy, moody, emotional, tense and anxious. Some cats are antisocial, giving no warmth to humans.

> *I am as much an individual as you are.*

Playful personality
Kittens cuddle and jostle with one another, often touching heads, as part of their normal social development. If they grow up without the opportunity of playing with other kittens, they do not develop a complete repertoire of cat behavior.

Outgoing individual
Playful batting and teasing is common between lively kittens. This sort of extrovert behavior during kittenhood often leads to similar behavior later in life, but it is not always possible to predict what type of personality a cat will develop.

Introverts and extroverts

Detailed experiments have shown that simply talking softly to kittens soon after they are born results in their growing up into more confident and independent adults. Such kittens even finish nursing sooner. Active kittens grow up to be high-energy individuals, while reserved kittens often mature into more retiring cats.

Apprehensive adult

(ABOVE) The introvert personality usually develops when the kitten lacks social contact. Although slow, quiet and less responsive than an extrovert, the cautious cat learns faster and is easier to train.

Dominant kitten

Physically dextrous, this extrovert kitten is paw-fighting with her sibling. The outgoing character is accentuated by gregarious play activity. Dominant kittens grow to become dominant cats as the personality trait is already present in the genes.

Shy puss

Watchful, tense and solitary, the introvert peeps out from behind an object. Lacking self-confidence and often fearful of or hostile toward people and other cats, the introvert type of character is established in the first weeks of life.

Reading Your Cat's Face

Watch my face closely and you might be able to tell my mood.

TO HUMAN EYES the cat's face is often inscrutable, but to other cats the slightest change in expression can mean many things. Cats are not a sociable species, so they have little need for cooperative signals. The position of the ears will usually give you the most accurate clue to your cat's mood. Unlike humans or dogs, the cat has not developed a facial expression or gesture, such as a friendly wave or a tail-wag, that is universally recognized as a greeting. A cat's face simply maintains a relaxed and alert look, even when truthfully pleased to see you. On the other hand, the cat's face is exquisitely expressive at telling you "Goodbye." Ears, eyes, whiskers and mouth leave you in no doubt as to the intended message.

Ears and eyes

There are over 20 muscles that control the position of the ears. When a cat is relaxed, greeting or exploring, the ears are held forward. Ears down indicate aggression; ears pinned back signal either fear or aggression, or both. Some cats, such as the Maine Coon, have extra ear tufts that accentuate ear position.

A cat's eyes also reveal mood. When your cat is completely relaxed, the eyes will shut. If frightened, the "fight-or-flight" response is automatically activated. The adrenalin then secreted causes the pupils to dilate.

The contented cat

(LEFT) Cats reveal their pleasure by half-closing their eyes in a reverie of contentment. This expression, with ears forward, is often accompanied by purring and is the ultimate sign of relaxation. The cat is free from any fear or worry.

The relaxed and alert cat

(ABOVE) This is the most common facial expression. It gives no "go away" signal and is used when cats greet us, when they demand attention, lie down, sit, stand, walk or trot. It communicates no danger to other cats.

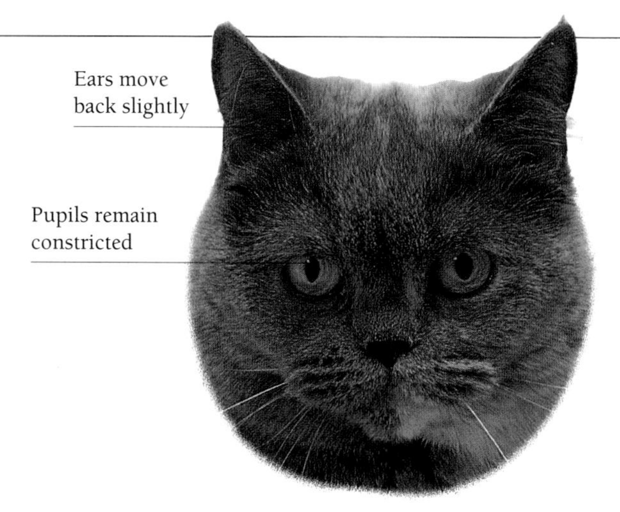

The ambivalent cat
Twitching ears mean your cat is uncertain of how she feels. Her mood can develop in any direction.

The fearful cat
When your cat is afraid, her ears fold down. In extreme fear, her ears will flatten completely.

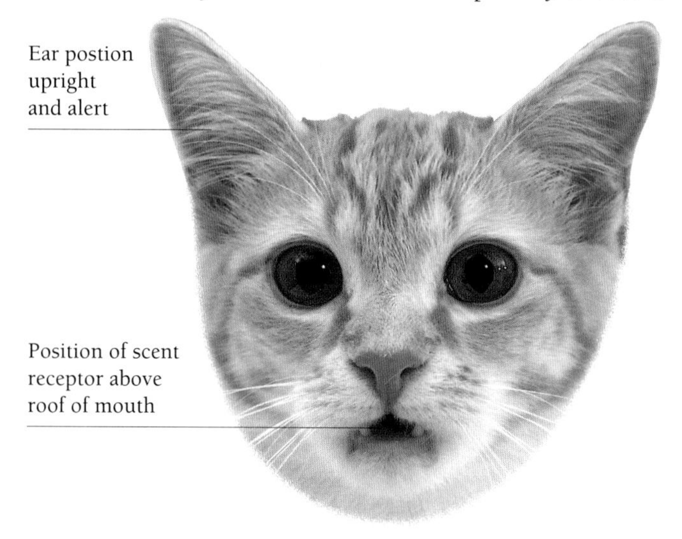

The "flehming" cat
This sneering expression occurs when a male picks up the scent of urine of a female in heat.

The curious cat
The inquisitive cat perks his ears forward to funnel in sounds. The pupils are slightly dilated.

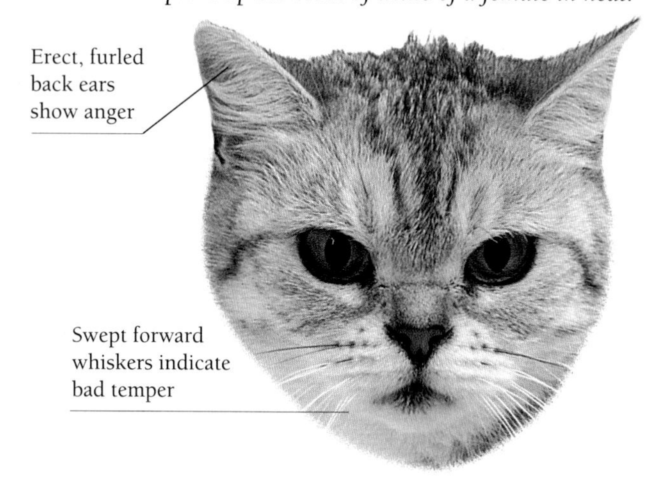

The angry cat
When a dominantly aggressive cat gets annoyed, the pupils remain constricted.

The aggressive cat
The pupils are dilated in fear. The cat opens her mouth wide to hiss, spit and show sharp teeth.

Cat Talk

YOUR CAT USES his voice to welcome you home, beg for food, demand attention, call for a mate, complain, threaten and protest. The mood your cat is in – angry, indignant, anxious, content – is also revealed in the voice. By the time kittens are 12 weeks old they have mastered the full range of adult cat vocabulary, which we know includes at least 16 different sounds. Cats can probably distinguish many more. Some individuals and some breeds, especially the Siamese, are more vocal than others.

> *I can say much more than you think I can.*

Motherly purr
(ABOVE) Her kittens busy suckling, the mother is in a relaxed position and purrs rhythmically with contentment. Exactly how a cat purrs is not yet fully understood, but it is thought to be a sound transferred from somewhere deep in the chest. As the voice box is not used, she can chirp at the same time.

Anxiety attack
The young kitten calls in distress. She makes this anxious cry, which is similar to a baby's, when she is hungry, cold or away from mother.

Extensive vocabulary

Cat language can be divided into three general sound categories: murmurs, vowels and high-intensity sounds. Murmurs include purring and the gentle chirping used in greeting or to express contentment. A mother cat will chirrup to beckon her kittens. Vowel sounds such as "meow," "mew," "MEE-ow" and "meOW" are made when the cat is demanding, complaining or bewildered. High-intensity sounds include the growl, angry wail, snarl, shriek of pain or fear, hiss, spit and the mating cry of the female.

Hissing and spitting
This cat arches her tongue in fear or anger to force out a jet of hot breath. Used to intimidate, the feel and smell of the hiss are just as important as the sound.

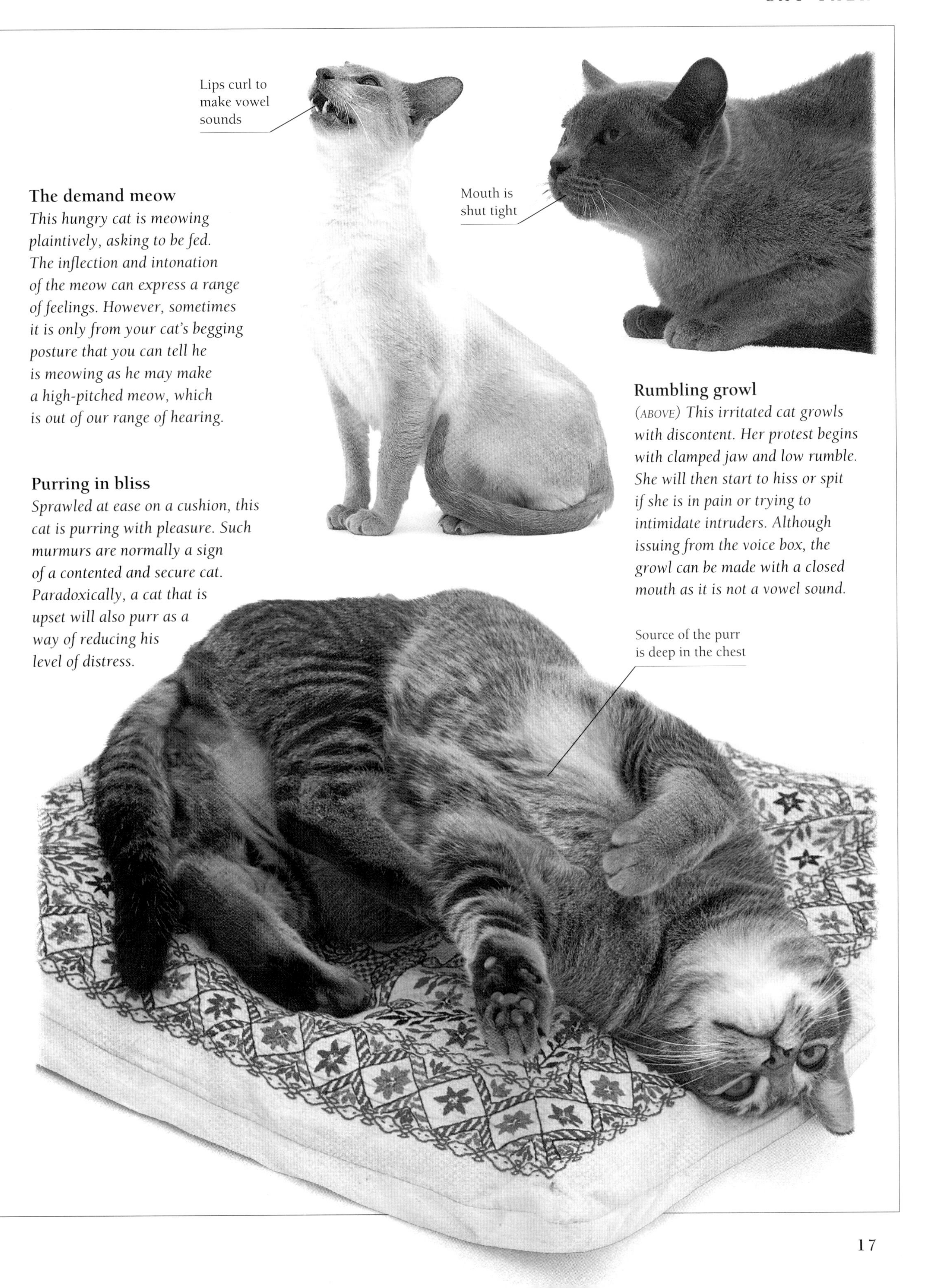

The demand meow

This hungry cat is meowing plaintively, asking to be fed. The inflection and intonation of the meow can express a range of feelings. However, sometimes it is only from your cat's begging posture that you can tell he is meowing as he may make a high-pitched meow, which is out of our range of hearing.

Rumbling growl

(ABOVE) *This irritated cat growls with discontent. Her protest begins with clamped jaw and low rumble. She will then start to hiss or spit if she is in pain or trying to intimidate intruders. Although issuing from the voice box, the growl can be made with a closed mouth as it is not a vowel sound.*

Purring in bliss

Sprawled at ease on a cushion, this cat is purring with pleasure. Such murmurs are normally a sign of a contented and secure cat. Paradoxically, a cat that is upset will also purr as a way of reducing his level of distress.

Being Defensive

YOUR CAT IS more concerned with defending her personal territory than with forming lasting friendships with other cats. Compared to a dog, she is a far less sociable creature and is remarkably adept at giving "go away" signals. When your cat feels that she has lost control of the situation or that she is under threat, the "fight-or-flight" response is usually triggered and adrenalin is released. Your cat will stand her ground and make a show of aggression. Her hackles rise, her back arches, her tail bristles, her pupils dilate, and she may hiss and spit. Even a terrified cat will put on a convincing display of defensive body language, although in many cases such behavior masks fear rather than genuine aggression.

Acting tough
(RIGHT) *With bristling tail, arched back, and hair standing on end, this cat is very scared but is trying to hide her fear with a display of aggressive body language. Presenting herself sideways for maximum impact, she appears to be considering an attack on the opposition.*

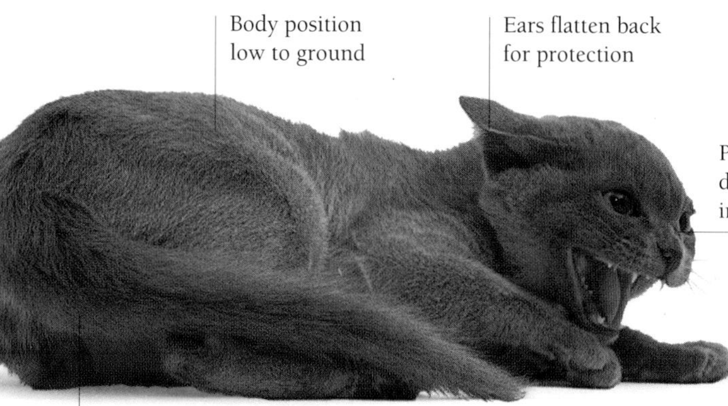

Weapons ready
(ABOVE) *Even though she is actually very frightened, this cat prepares to act aggressively. Hissing, she starts to roll over so that teeth and claws are bared, ready to defend herself.*

Poised for action
(RIGHT) *This terrified cat is attempting to hold her ground. Stimulated by adrenalin, her pupils have dilated and she gives a direct stare to intimidate. Puffed up to a larger size, she is staging a dramatic display of bravado.*

Defensive display
(RIGHT) *With dilated pupils, flattened ears, bristling whiskers and thumping tail, this cat threatens with his voice, and is prepared for an attack.*

On the Offense

THE ABILITY TO BLUFF with confidence is an absolute necessity for the cat that takes an offensive stance. There is no fixed pecking order in the cat world, so the tendency to act offensively or defensively varies according to the circumstance in which your cat finds himself. A cat in its own territory or holding the higher ground over an adversary – perhaps on a rooftop – will display offensive body language. Feeling confident, he is able to maintain full control of himself. Since, in this instance, the cat feels genuinely secure, the pupils do not dilate because the "fight-or-flight" response is not activated, as it would be in a frightened, defensive cat.

Secure at the top
While this cat sits on the roof he dominates all others below him. Exuding confidence with his head, whiskers, perked ears and smooth coat, the cat keeps a lookout for intruders. He may use his height advantage to ambush or attack.

Natural response
Crouched forward to hold her ground, the mother protects her young. The forward ear position and undilated pupils show that she is in control.

Ears perked forward show confidence

Thick cheek ruffs make the tomcat appear larger

Forelimbs prepared for a forward spring

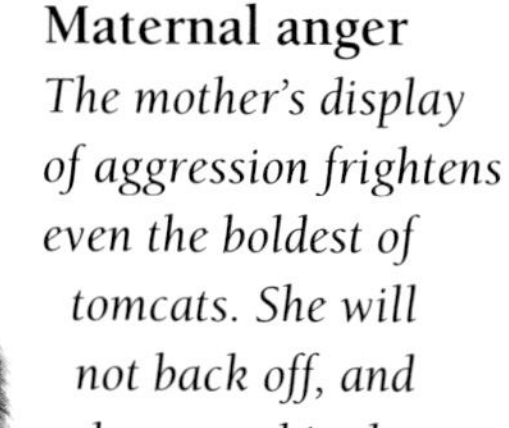

Maternal anger
The mother's display of aggression frightens even the boldest of tomcats. She will not back off, and threatens him by hissing and spitting offensively. If he does not retreat, she will spring forward.

Look out! I'm in charge around here.

Dominant stance
Although watched by the tom on the roof, this cat is not frightened. With his well-developed sense of balance, he leans confidently over the post. Glaring down at the cat on the fence without worrying about falling off, he warns his adversary not to come any closer.

Smooth body fur signals confidence

Forward ears look assertive

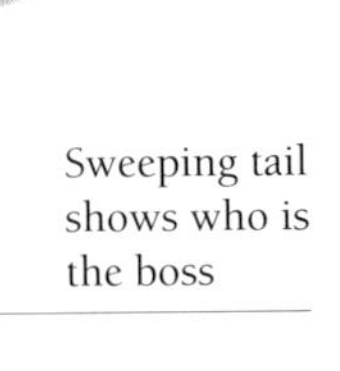

Sweeping tail shows who is the boss

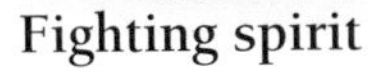

Taut face muscles prepared for attack

Fighting spirit
(ABOVE) With ears slightly furled, the confident but angry cat opens her mouth wide to hiss or spit. The tongue is folded to funnel out a shot of hot breath. The lips curl back revealing sharp teeth, emphasizing the snarl.

Pricked, furled back ears display determination to stand ground

Direct eye contact indicates bravery

Facing a rival
By putting her head forward, this bold cat refuses to be intimidated by the cat on the high ground. However, the erect fur on the tail is a sure sign that she is a little frightened.

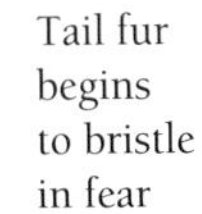

Tail fur begins to bristle in fear

Withdrawn forepaws ready for action

Marking Territory

THE FELINE LANDOWNER routinely leaves messages to tell other cats who owns the territory. This involves making regular patrols of his home ground and marking important hunting, feeding and resting places. The marks he leaves can be either seen or smelled. The cat that rubs himself up against you is not simply showing affection. He is transferring his body odor, claiming you as part of his territory. When a cat has the freedom of the garden, he will scratch fence posts and tree trunks. Indoors, the cat may claw at sofas and chairs to make his mark visible. Both males and females can spray urine, even if they have been neutered, and a dominant tomcat will leave his droppings unburied as a combined visual and scent marker.

Staking a claim
(LEFT) *Urine spraying is a marking behavior and is completely different than emptying the bladder. The cat backs up to the object it intends to mark and, with a quivering tail, squirts urine straight out backward.*

The indoor cat
(ABOVE) *Most females and neutered cats are content with a small indoor territory, but they still make marks. This neutered female has a chair that she stoutly defends.*

The face rub
The cat rubs her face against the fence to mark it. Scent from the cheek glands is transferred to the wood.

It smells as if my neighbor has been here today. I'd better mark it as mine again.

Scratching posts
The ears fold back and an almost trancelike gaze comes over the cat as she reaches up to claw at the highest point possible. Wood is a favorite surface because it is not slippery. The scratches, which can be seen from a distance, are usually made in prominent sites.

The routine patrol
The cat must make fresh markings every day using bodily secretions. The marks left do not frighten away other cats. Rather, they tell intruders on the territory how recently the owner passed through.

Patrolling the Home Beat

MOST PET CATS adopt their owners' fences as their own territorial boundaries. Because cats are so successful at adapting to human ways, surprisingly few problems arise from this arrangement. The size of a territory depends upon the cat's age, sexual status and personality. Females and neutered cats are usually content with fairly small land rights, whereas tomcats feel the need to patrol and defend much larger territories – often ten times the area of a female's. Feral tomcats and cats without owners also establish a hunting range connected to their home territory by specific boundary lines and pathways.

Time to survey my domain.

Creating land rights

If your cat does not have sufficient room to maneuver, he will remedy the situation by appropriating a neighbor's lawn. He will stake it out with strategic droppings. Neutering dramatically reduces a cat's territorial demand because the sex hormone is one of the factors that drives the cat to create and defend territory.

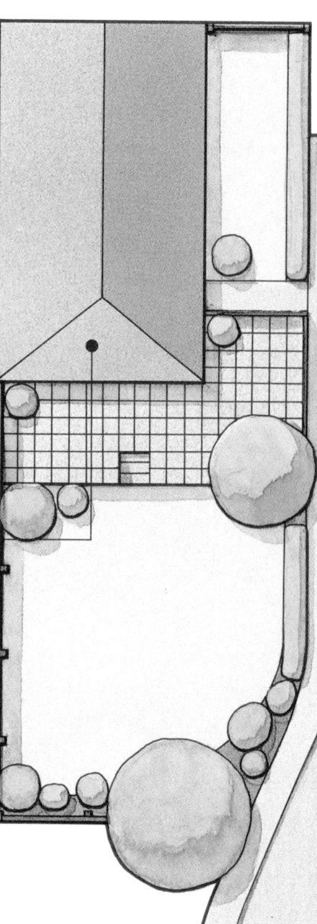

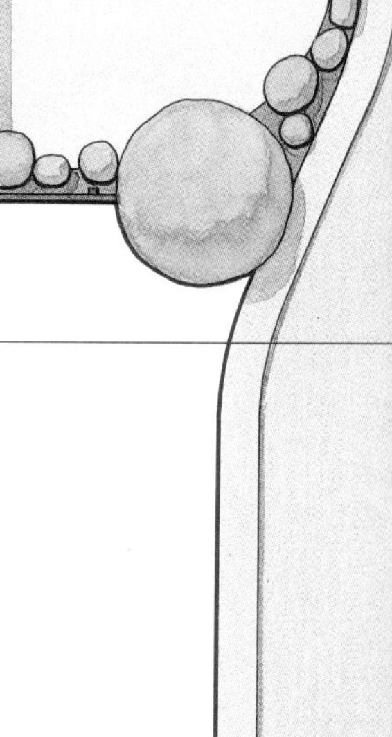

Holding the high ground
(ABOVE) *Regardless of which is the most dominant when two cats meet, the one that holds the highest ground has a distinct advantage. This is one reason why cats enjoy patrolling rooftops. From a height, your cat can survey his territory and shout insults at intruders.*

Patrolling from above
(RIGHT) *Cats live in both the vertical and the horizontal world. Tomcats tend to spend more time policing their territory than females.*

Preserving land
(LEFT) *Taking their cue from human territory markers, cats are often content to remain within one back yard but will vigorously defend that patch against other feline intruders. However, your cat's range may extend to more than one human territory.*

Adapting to human lifestyle
Many cats are content to live their lives indoors with us where there is no need to forage for food and where we "protect" the home territory. Even so, indoor cats will still assume ownership and defend a favorite spot, such as a chair.

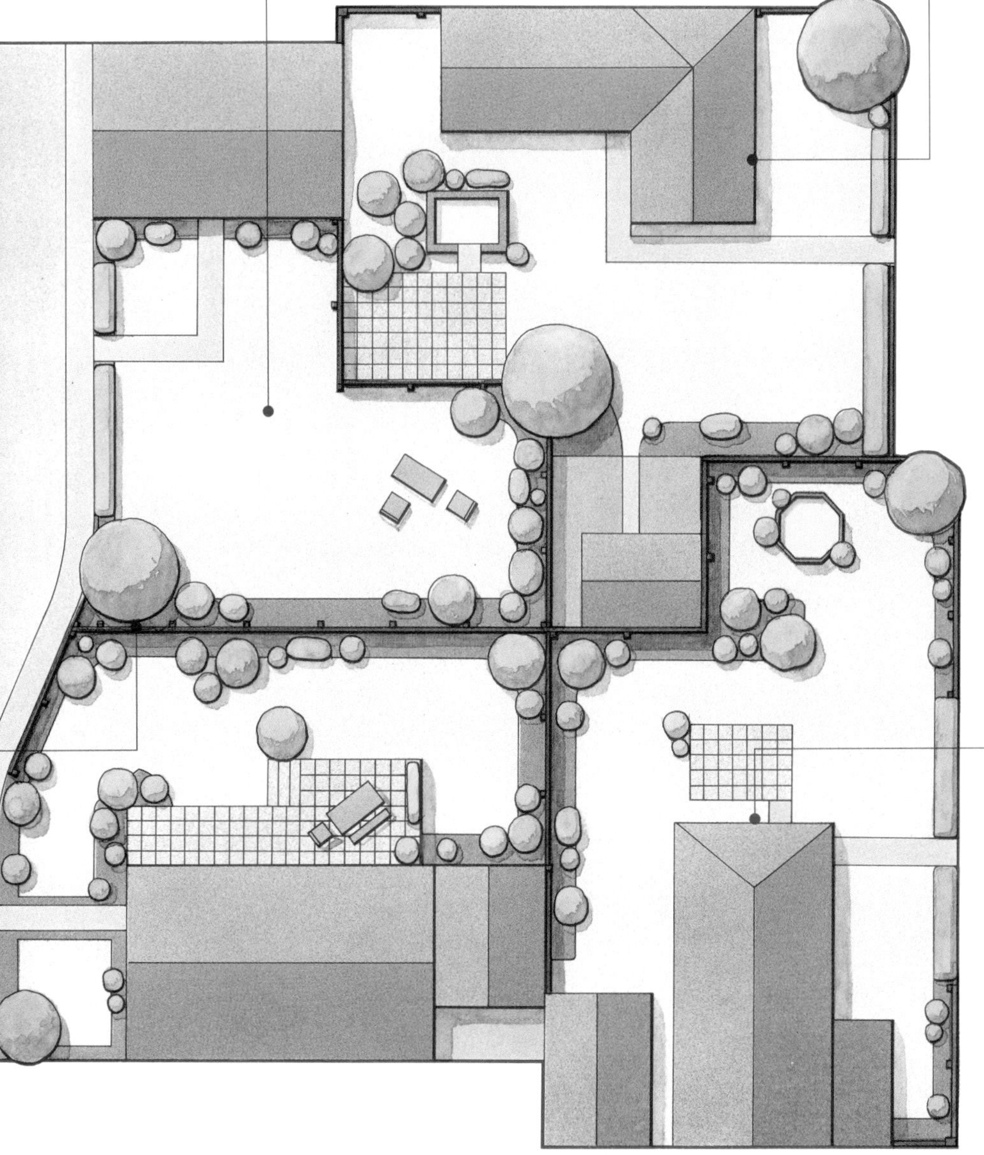

Protecting the ideal home
(ABOVE) *A perfect home territory provides a reliable food supply and safe resting areas that are always accessible. The cat flap ensures your cat's independence, so he can come and go at will.*

Cat Relationships

Vital contact
Daily stroking ensures that young kittens will develop into adults that enjoy the company of human beings.

Cats are ideal companions. They are quiet, reliable, self-cleaning and independent. They always make good listeners, are perfect creatures for cuddling and have low maintenance costs. Breeding practices have not led to a dramatically altered cat anatomy, as is often the case with many new dog breeds, and so cats have comparatively few physical problems.

Cats satisfy a deep-seated human need to nurture and care for living things, and at the same time they are content to depend entirely upon us for their own survival. Cats are happy to remain dependents, permitting us to act as their surrogate mothers, providing them with food, protection, warmth and security. In many ways, cats and humans have the perfect symbiotic relationship.

Freedom to move
A cat flap gives your cat security while satisfying his need to explore outdoors.

Making friends
These three unrelated kittens will be lifelong friends because they were introduced before the age of seven weeks.

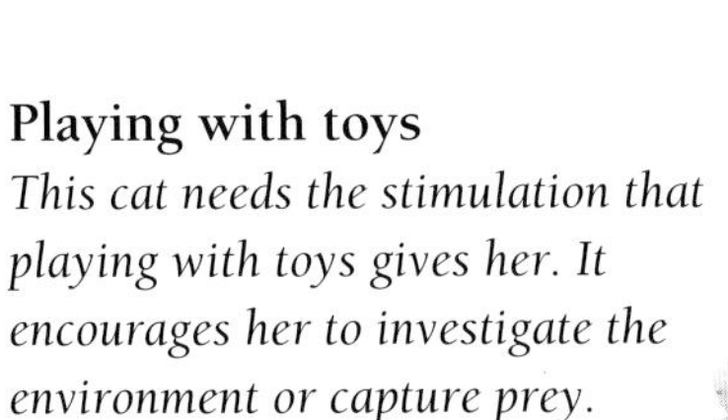

Playing with toys
This cat needs the stimulation that playing with toys gives her. It encourages her to investigate the environment or capture prey.

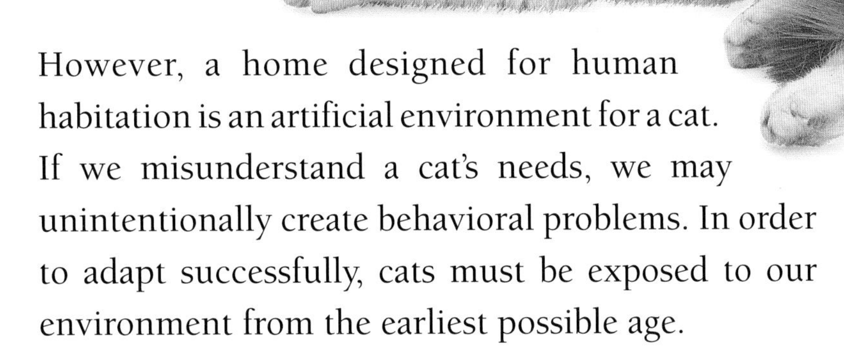

However, a home designed for human habitation is an artificial environment for a cat. If we misunderstand a cat's needs, we may unintentionally create behavioral problems. In order to adapt successfully, cats must be exposed to our environment from the earliest possible age.

Treating problems
A squirt from a plant sprayer can break your cat of bad habits, such as scratching your furniture or clawing the curtains.

The desire to define and possess territory exists in all cats, whether they live in an urban apartment or in a remote rural area. When a cat has limited access to the great outdoors, we should provide him with articles that can be scratched and a toilet area that is appropriate, private and suitably placed. Cats are, of course, highly adaptable creatures, but we should still repay their friendship by providing them with a safe and comforting home that caters to every conceivable cat requirement.

Comfort behaviors
This Siamese kitten is a wool-sucker. The problem is much more common in Siamese than in other cats and is probably caused by selective breeding.

Your Best Friend

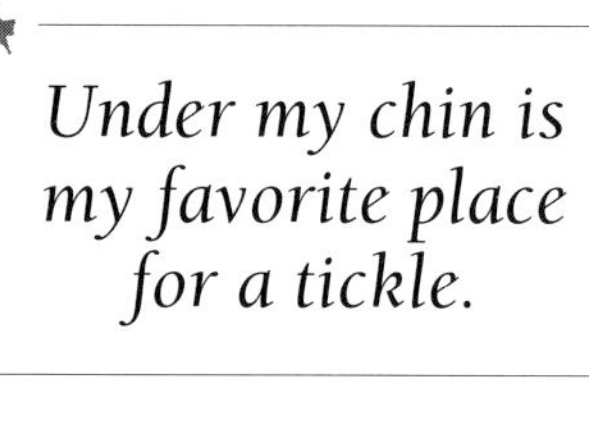

Under my chin is my favorite place for a tickle.

THE SATISFACTION WE derive from caring for living things is at the root of our survival as a species. It is also the reason why so many of us find such pleasure in sharing our homes with cats. Curiously, cats may be even better than children in fulfilling our need to nurture: they never grow up and are always dependent on us. Stroking them indulges our desire for closeness. Talking, touching and eye-to-eye contact create an intimacy that is sometimes easier to maintain with a cat than with another person. Cats provide us with a reassuring constancy in our lives, which we like to interpret as loyalty.

Tongue leaves territorial saliva on human skin

Kitten is stimulated by gentle tickling

Mutual satisfaction

Feeling secure, the mother cat licks your hand as she would her own kittens. In return, you take pleasure from stroking the fur under her chin. Children, too, benefit from the affection engendered within a family for a pet cat.

Intimate relationship

Stroking your cat is very relaxing. Lying on your chest, enjoying the caresses, he makes a perfect listener. He sees you as a mother substitute, displaying none of the competitive behavior that normally occurs between two cats.

Direct eye contact demonstrates trust

Learning to socialize

(RIGHT) Kittens are "socialized" when they are handled and played with. The child also learns that there is a limit to the length of time during which they enjoy being handled.

Secure footing
(ABOVE) The kittens feel most secure on the ground and are happy to be petted. Stroking the chin satisfies the kitten's need to leave her scent.

Lap of luxury
(ABOVE) Lying on your warm lap, your cat's state of arousal is diminished. She kneads your leg with her claws, which is a comfort behavior, and shows her appreciation by arching her neck back to try to give you a friendly "head rub."

Your Cat's Best Friend

FOR A CAT, humans make good cat substitutes. In many ways cats enjoy warmer, more convivial relations with us than they do with other felines. Humans are almost ideal social companions as they do not represent any kind of threat to a cat. We do not compete for food, territory or sexual supremacy – factors that interfere in the relationships between cats. When raised in close proximity to us, cats look upon humans as being "feline" enough to be treated as fellow cats while being sufficiently different not to be a danger. A lasting dependency and friendship can develop between a cat and a human being, with the cat regarding its owner as an all-powerful, all-providing mother.

"You may not be my mother, but you still groom me, feed me and care for me."

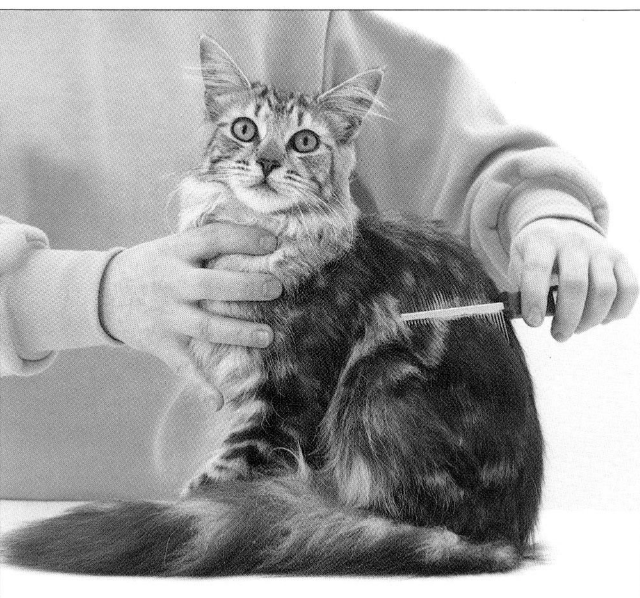

Grooming time
(RIGHT) *Long-haired breeds may need help to keep their coats in condition and to prevent them from becoming matted and tangled. This Maine Coon sits still while she is groomed with a comb. Most cats enjoy grooming as the sensation is similar to that experienced as kittens, when their mother licked their fur.*

Nose activated by smell of food

Meal time
The mother cat reaches up to ask for her food and smells it curiously. The begging action is also displayed by a kitten when the mother returns to the litter with a mouse.

Parent power

Cats are inherently lazy, always taking the easy option. When we provide food and shelter for our pet cat, we create a dependency that is similar to a kitten's total reliance on his mother. An adult feral cat is preoccupied with concerns of territory, competition and mating. Your pet cat does not have these worries and so retains a certain youthfulness, looking to you to provide for him just like a mother. Selective breeding has increased this dependency. Cats with long coats, for example, would not survive without help with grooming. Breeders are even selecting for temperament. For example, by choosing the aesthetic comforter in preference to the mouser, the floppy and affectionate Ragdoll breed has been created.

Staying healthy

Cats depend in part on humans to help them maintain their health, so visiting the vet is an occasional necessity. Train your cat from an early age to travel in a cat basket. Always grasp your cat firmly when putting her into the basket.

The dependent feline

Reaching up, the cat sniffs your hand in greeting. She tries to get as close as possible to give you a "head rub," the cat's natural way of saying hello. Human interaction has perpetuated the dependency of the kitten on its mother. The result is a domestic cat that actively seeks out human companionship, relying on us for fundamental needs.

Being Handled

YOUR CAT IS not instinctively gregarious and can resent incorrect handling. She is a graceful, dignified, clean, independent, sensuous creature, so it is natural to respect her and often impossible to resist touching her. A cat unfamiliar with the sensation of being picked up will allow you to do this only if she feels relaxed, comfortable and secure. A cat that was not stroked as a kitten will fiercely resist any attempts at handling.

This kitten is relaxed because it is correctly supported

"Hold me correctly and I'll be relaxed."

Correct handling
(ABOVE) *Support the kitten's hindquarters with the palm of one hand while cradling the forelimbs and head with the other. Never pick up a kitten by the scruff of the neck as its mother does, because this can damage her fragile body. A kitten must be handled frequently to ensure that she enjoys being stroked later in life.*

Cat shows pleasure at being rubbed firmly behind the ears

The head rub
(LEFT) *By rubbing her head against your hand, the cat leaves her marking scent. Unable to groom behind the ears with her tongue, the cat likes being caressed here. Your strokes are similar to the licks her mother once gave her.*

Medicine time
(ABOVE) *A cat will try to swat or bite you when you give it a pill. Hold the head firmly with one hand and flex it back to open the mouth. Drop the pill in and then shut the mouth. Rub the throat to encourage the cat to swallow the pill.*

Stroking a cat

Your cat finds stroking pleasurable because the sensation is similar to that of grooming. However, this type of physical contact is not a natural adult cat behavior, so it must be included in your kitten's socialization period.

Handling time

Kittens should be handled for at least 40 minutes each day from two weeks of age onward. The more handling they receive when they are young, the more they will actively enjoy future handling. However, constant petting may produce mixed emotions. Cats can reveal their ambivalence by suddenly biting your hand and then coming back to ask for more affection. An aggressive response is most likely to occur when you rub the cat's belly because it is the least protected part of a cat's body and never mutually groomed.

Supporting hands
Pick the cat up with one hand on its chest behind the forepaws and the other under the hindquarters. This supports the full weight and avoids any discomfort to the legs or rib cage.

Correctly handled, the young cat remains relaxed

The handover
(RIGHT) The limp tail and hanging paws show that the cat is relaxed as it is handed over to the girl. The child must have the cat firmly in both hands before you release your hold.

Sitting comfortably
For a cat, being cradled is unnatural and unfamiliar. Preferring to be upright, the cat will tolerate being held like this only when it feels completely secure and relaxed with the girl.

Sheathed claws mean kitten is not alarmed

Limp tail shows cat is at ease

Crooked arm provides security

Roaming Free

Although your cat is among the world's most prolific sleepers, he also needs frequent activity. One of his favorite natural pastimes is to make rounds of his territory. He will instinctively practice his hunting skills and leave marks to stake out his domain. If he is denied access to the outdoors, he may spend hours at the window watching the world go by. When he sees something that excites or distresses him, he might back up to the furniture, raise his tail and quiver. Spraying urine inside your home is the way he demonstrates his frustration when he is cooped up. This behavioral problem almost always occurs when your cat's access to the outside is limited, or if there are too many cats sharing your home.

Living indoors
(ABOVE) This indoor cat concentrates on the outside world through the window. If he spots a bird, he may chatter his teeth and swish his tail. He could become agitated if his natural activity is restricted too much.

Tail maintains balance

Using a litter box

If you cannot give your cat access to the great outdoors, you need to provide litter in a box in a secluded place. Part of your cat's natural behavior is to bury her droppings, so she is already receptive to the principle of using a litter box. She will become accustomed to the odor of the litter and the texture of it under foot and may object, refusing to use it, if you change the type of litter.

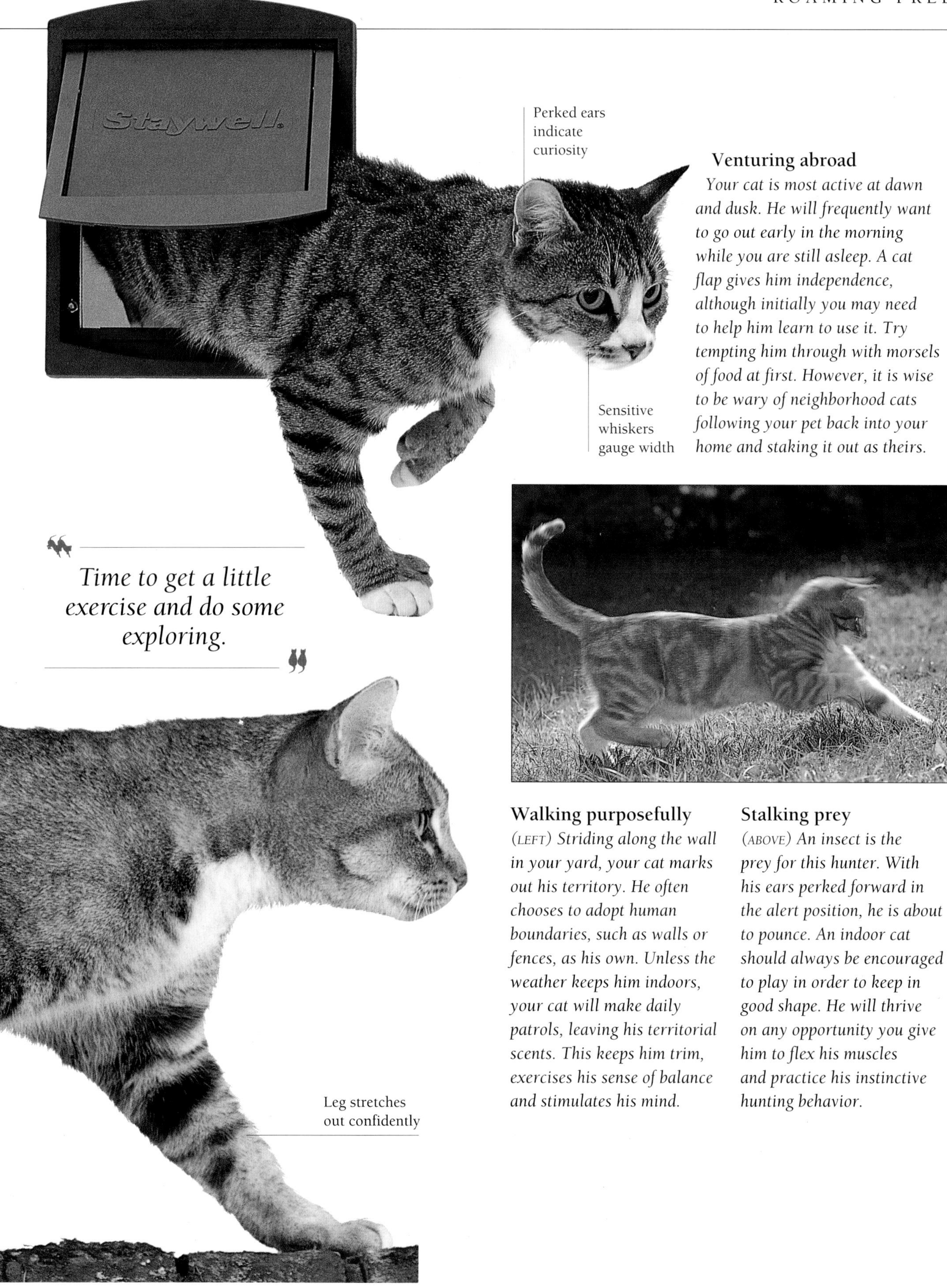

Venturing abroad

Your cat is most active at dawn and dusk. He will frequently want to go out early in the morning while you are still asleep. A cat flap gives him independence, although initially you may need to help him learn to use it. Try tempting him through with morsels of food at first. However, it is wise to be wary of neighborhood cats following your pet back into your home and staking it out as theirs.

Time to get a little exercise and do some exploring.

Walking purposefully

(LEFT) *Striding along the wall in your yard, your cat marks out his territory. He often chooses to adopt human boundaries, such as walls or fences, as his own. Unless the weather keeps him indoors, your cat will make daily patrols, leaving his territorial scents. This keeps him trim, exercises his sense of balance and stimulates his mind.*

Stalking prey

(ABOVE) *An insect is the prey for this hunter. With his ears perked forward in the alert position, he is about to pounce. An indoor cat should always be encouraged to play in order to keep in good shape. He will thrive on any opportunity you give him to flex his muscles and practice his instinctive hunting behavior.*

Being Sociable

YOUR CAT CAN get along with a wide variety of other animals, as well as those of her own species. Provided a young kitten is introduced between two and seven weeks old, a lasting friendship with another cat or a different species can be established successfully. We always tend to think of the stereotype of dog chasing cat, but in reality many dogs are intimidated by cats. Make sure the first few meetings between a young kitten and potential soulmate are sensitively handled, taking care not to trespass on an existing pet's territory, and the kitten will enjoy the companionship later in life. The resulting friendship is a unique behavioral feature of domestic rather than feral cats.

Agitated expression shows insecurity

“Who goes there – friend or foe?”

First encounters
(ABOVE) *Introduced to a dog for the first time, this kitten is terrified. Her fur stands on end and she adopts a defensive stance. Provided that the meeting is not provocative, the next time they see each other the kitten should be less scared.*

Well-socialized kitten
Not at all inhibited by the dog, this kitten met dogs frequently when she was young so her fear of larger animals is diminished. If you want your pets to be friends, make sure that the kitten mixes with dogs when between the ages of two and seven weeks.

Naturally fluffy tail is relaxed and limp

Intimidating the stranger

This dominant adult cat defends her home from the new kitten. Hissing and spitting, her paw is raised, about to swat the youngster. Nervous, he pulls back, too inexperienced to understand what is happening. His muted response is confused.

Making friends

(LEFT) *These kittens amuse themselves, playing with the wool and each other. As the period during which kittens can bond starts early and is over so quickly, it is best to acquire several kittens at once if you plan to become a multicat family.*

Playing with humans

(BELOW) *Chewing and pulling on shoelaces, these kittens discover that humans make very good playmates. Neither kitten is fearful, but the one lying on his side, with his tail up, shows the beginnings of defensive behavior as he grabs with his forepaws and kicks with his hindlegs.*

Learning to share territory

Initially, a resident pet may not be willing to share territory with a new kitten. To make the introduction as smooth as possible, let the resident dog or cat sniff the sleeping newcomer.

If you are getting a kitten from a breeder, make sure that he or she has already experienced social contact with other species. After seven weeks of age, the kitten can no longer make social bonds, so it will be very difficult for the cat ever to be friends with other pets. It is important to remember that a kitten that is not scared of your dog may be at risk from strange dogs.

Exercising Mind and Body

UNLESS YOUR CAT'S energy can be channeled in a positive way, he may become destructive. After all, he never has to worry about where his next meal is coming from, so there is no need for any real hunting or stalking. The frustrated cat that has excess energy to burn will chew your plants, scratch your furniture, tear your carpets and climb the curtains.

He may even go berserk for half an hour, running maniacally back and forth across the room or round the perimeter, doing the "wall of death" – strange behavior for a cat, normally so lazy a creature! Some cats develop the annoying habit of sucking wool, usually a sign of premature weaning. In order to prevent these problems occurring, ensure that your cat is always mentally stimulated and has plenty of opportunity for exercise.

Watch out – I'm going to create havoc!

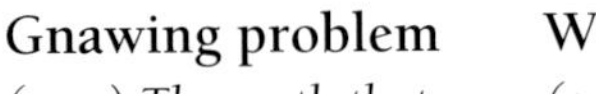

Gnawing problem
(LEFT) *The myth that cats only eat grass when they are unwell is just that. Although they are carnivores, many cats often nibble grass. Inside, this cat tears at a house plant instead. Make sure that none of your plants are poisonous.*

Wool sucking
(ABOVE) *If your young kittens suck wool, or even you, they could have been weaned too soon from their mothers. Siamese may start sucking after they are around six months old, but this is usually a genetically linked behavioral problem.*

Stimulating your cat

Toys provide a practical outlet through which cats can exhaust themselves. They need not imitate prey specifically, but should encourage activities such as scratching, chasing and batting. Toys that move erratically are often favored as they arouse the cat's curiosity.

Scratching posts

(LEFT) *Your cat needs to be able to scratch. Very often after waking, a cat has the urge to claw something, just as we like to stretch. Providing a good post will prevent damage to furniture.*

Moving target

Standing up on his hind legs, with his tail straight out for balance, this cat is inquisitive about the toy. He will investigate it by feeling, sniffing, tasting and poking. As it swings back and forth, it will provide him with endless hours of amusement.

Training Your Cat

ALTHOUGH WE SELDOM notice it, cats are constantly training themselves. If, for example, your cat raids the garbage can successfully, he learns this is rewarding. However, rewards such as food or affection do not work well when training cats out of bad habits. Surprise, never involving pain, is the best way to overcome most of your feline's behavioral problems.

Bean bag
Throw a small bean bag near your cat if he attempts, for example, to climb the curtains.

Aluminum foil
(ABOVE) If your cat toilets outside the litter box, spread aluminum foil on the area. Cats do not like the feel of it under their feet and will learn to prefer the litter box.

Mothballs
(ABOVE) To prevent your cat from digging up the houseplants, spread mothballs (cats hate the smell) on the soil. Make sure the mothballs are kept away from children.

Plant sprayer
Cats dislike jets of water. Use a small sprayer or water gun to squirt your cat if she claws at the carpet or curtains.

Noisemakers
A noisemaker is an alternative surprise tactic. The clanging frightens the cat.

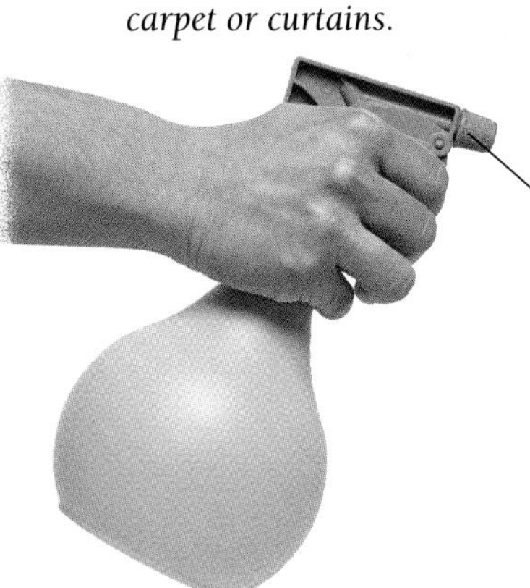

Select nozzle for an intensive jet of water

Punishing routine
When you see your cat misbehaving and the spray bottle is handy, simply fire the water the moment the cat claws the plant. Do not shout; the cat may begin to associate the punishment with you.

> *Oh, no! I knew I wouldn't get away with it!*

Correcting directly
(RIGHT) *If your cat uses you as a scratching post, or sucks at your clothes, gently tap him on the nose, but never inflict pain. Dominant cats often pat other cats if they step out of line. Admonish your cat in this way only when he has misbehaved directly toward you.*

Retaliating first
(LEFT) *You may be absent when your cat decides to misbehave. In this instance, it is necessary to create "traps" that will discipline him instantly. For example, cover the kitchen work surface with pots and pans that are bound to be knocked over when he jumps onto it, or set mousetraps under paper around the base of chewable plants.*

Springing the trap
(BELOW) *In order to approach the foliage, this cat must step onto the surrounding paper. This provides enough pressure to spring the mousetrap.*

Caring for Your Cat

THE DOMESTIC CAT is a highly adaptable African carnivore that has found living with humans to its liking. We may find some of its natural behaviors, such as territory-marking and toilet habits, socially unacceptable, but when offered the right equipment and given correct training, most cats can channel their natural habits into more domesticated directions. They will readily learn to use litter trays, scratch on special posts and eat food prepared by us.

PREPARING THE TRAY

TYPES OF LITTER

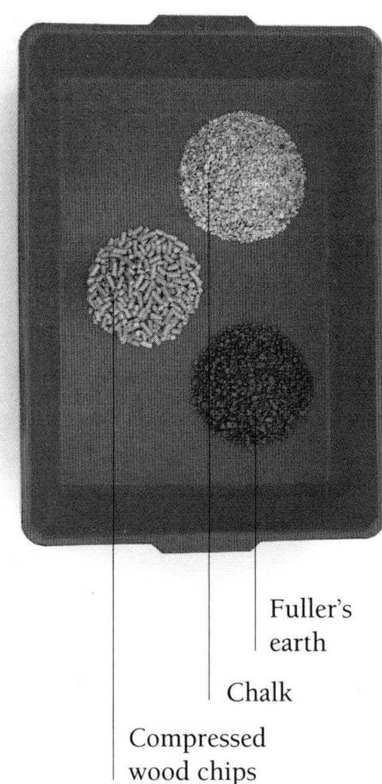

Choosing litter
(LEFT) Line the tray with a plastic bag before filling it with litter. For your cat, the most important quality of litter is how it feels under foot. Your cat may often develop a preference for one texture over another and may be unwilling to switch to a new type of litter.

Granting freedom
(ABOVE) Your cat's natural desire to climb and wander is so powerful that most want to venture outdoors. They can crawl through tight spaces and have no qualms about learning to squeeze through a cat flap once it is understood that the flap leads outside.

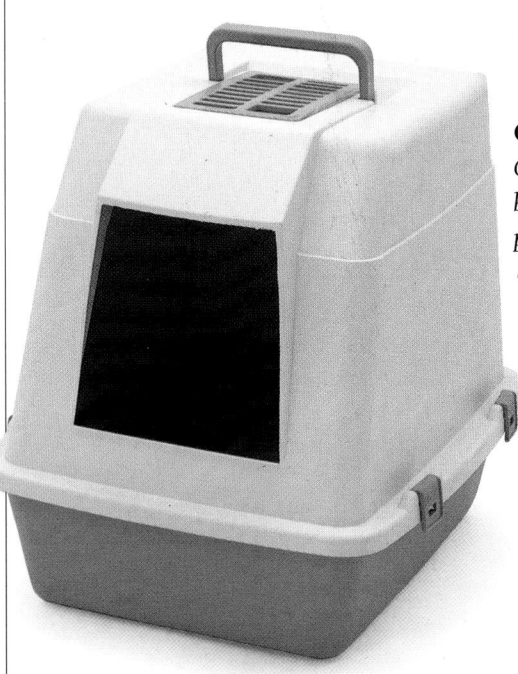

Creating privacy
Cats are innately litter-box trained and most prefer quiet and private areas. Covered litter boxes will meet your cat's requirements for security. Some come with built-in odor filters.

Selecting a diet
Although soft food might seem to be a more natural option, many cats prefer crunchy food. Eating the bones of their rodent prey is normal, and chewing on dry, pellets of food might simply duplicate that eating pattern. Although many cats seem to obtain sufficient water from the food they eat, it is advisable to supply your cat with a handy source of fresh water.

Simple rewards

The desired end result of training your cat is to redirect his natural behaviors into habits more suited to your home environment. Praise works with dogs, but cats do not respond well to it. Caring for your cat means providing him with the necessities of life – for him, these are rewards in themselves.

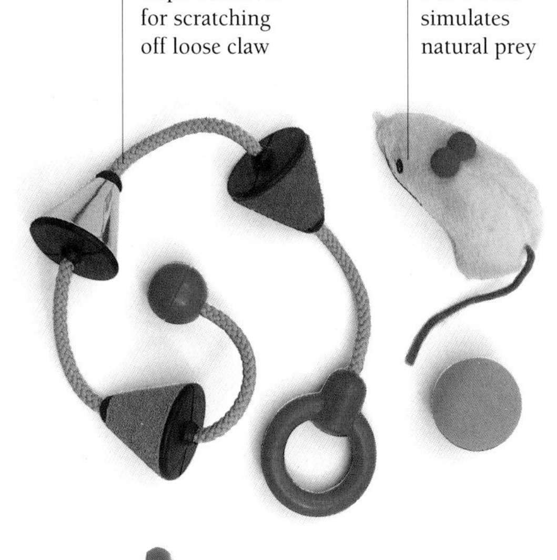

Traveling baskets
(ABOVE) *Your cat may learn to associate a traveling basket with a trip to the veterinarian. Using the basket as a warm, secluded bed at home helps to train your cat to associate the carrier with pleasant experiences.*

Exhilarating activity
(RIGHT) *Toys provide mental and physical stimulation. Lightweight balls will be batted; mouse-shaped toys encourage stalking and hunting activities. More sophisticated toys stimulate the senses of hearing and touch as well as sight.*

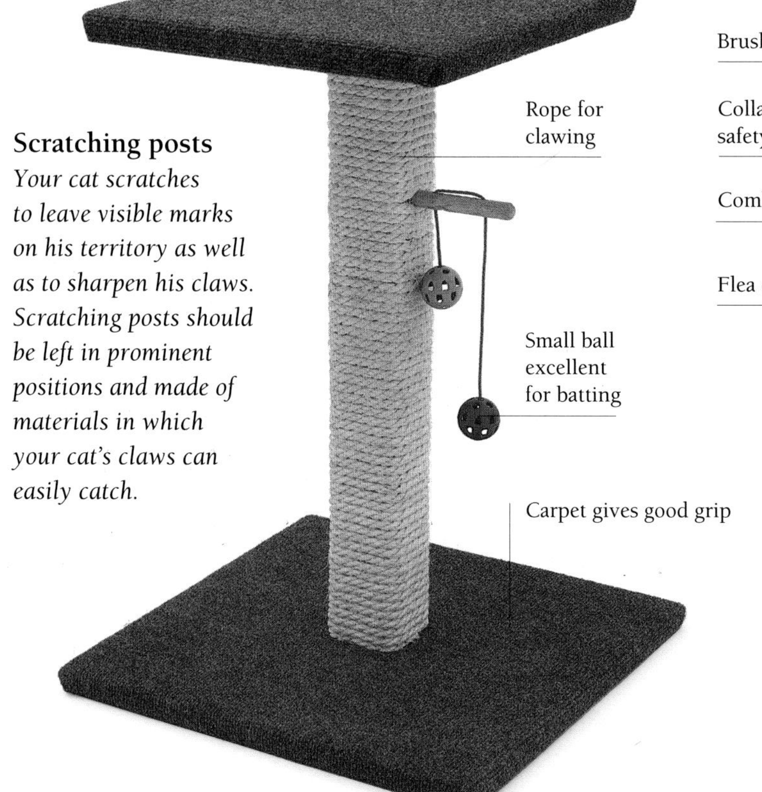

Scratching posts
Your cat scratches to leave visible marks on his territory as well as to sharpen his claws. Scratching posts should be left in prominent positions and made of materials in which your cat's claws can easily catch.

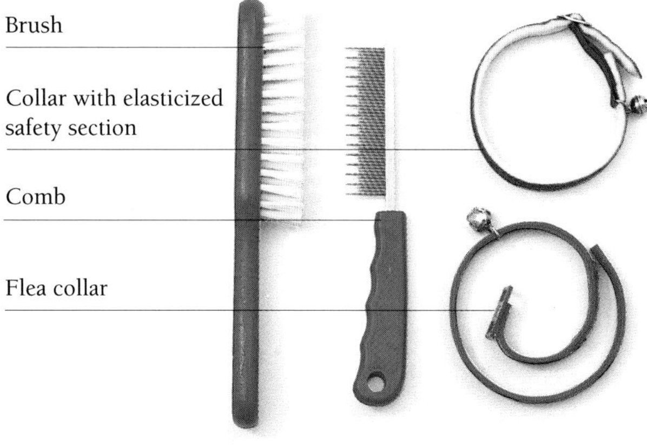

Brushes, combs and collars
Domestic cats, particularly longhairs, need extra grooming from you in addition to the grooming they give themselves and each other. If your cat's coat gets very dirty, you may need to give him a wet or dry bath. Also, ask your vet to show you how to trim claws.

HAVING A FAMILY

Total dependency
Licked dry, this kitten relies solely on mother for all his needs.

Feeling relaxed
Her distended abdomen indicates that this calm mother-to-be is close to delivering her kittens.

TRANQUILLITY, SERENITY AND dignified calm surround the mother cat before, during and after the birth of her kittens. From the moment she appears pregnant a few weeks after mating until the time she weans her kittens when they are around eight weeks old, her temperament and behavior are strongly influenced by progesterone, the hormone of pregnancy and lactation. She becomes calmer, is less likely to fight, appears more relaxed and may show greater affection toward humans. As birth approaches, and then for several weeks after the birth, she does not wander far from home, preferring to stay close to her nest.

Breathing space
Giving birth is a tiring process. This cat pants with exhaustion between deliveries.

Progesterone suppresses her fears and relaxes her, making her feel more secure. At the same time, however, it allows the unique maternal type

Rapid development
Although the senses develop quickly, this kitten needs his mother to stimulate his body functions.

Huddling together
The kittens snuggle together for warmth as their mother goes off in search of food.

First breaths
The mother's raspy tongue removes all birth fluids and stimulates the newborn into breathing.

of aggression to develop. If a nursing mother thinks that her kittens are at risk from an intruder, she will first threaten, then launch, a terrifying attack. Unlike other forays, there is no bluff involved in maternal aggression. The attack is maintained until the cause of her anxiety leaves the vicinity of her nest. Even the most powerful tomcat has a healthy respect for the ferocity of a female protecting her young.

Maternal care is overwhelmingly important in the life cycle of the cat. In fact, cats could be classified as a truly matriarchal species. The survival of each kitten depends solely upon females. Although the natural mother is primarily responsible for the care of her young, other females will feed and protect the kittens in her absence. Neither the father of the litter nor any other males assist in looking after the newborn.

Sole provider
For the first three weeks of life, this mother will furnish her kittens with milk, warmth, contact and comfort.

Expecting Kittens

YOUR PREGNANT CAT should be allowed to lead a normal life. During the early stages of pregnancy, it is safe for her to venture out and hunt. Climbing can be dangerous when she is greatly distended because the weight of the unborn kittens alters her center of gravity and affects her balance. She will be innately more careful, but the experienced mother adapts better to changes caused by pregnancy. An increased level of progesterone brings on "maternal behavior," and the expectant mother spends more time relaxing. Near full-term her estrogen level rises and she will begin searching for a nesting site.

Sitting comfortably
(BELOW) The expectant mother adopts a prone position. Stretched out like this, the load in her abdomen is more evenly distributed and is supported by the floor. Although cautious, she remains normally active until the weight of the litter and the hormonal changes in her body gradually cause her to slow down and rest more of the time.

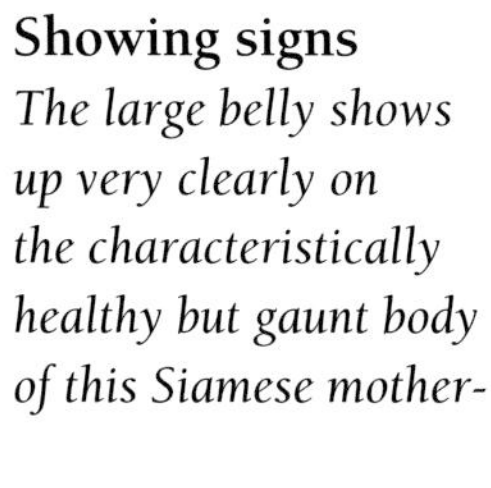

Showing signs
The large belly shows up very clearly on the characteristically healthy but gaunt body of this Siamese mother-to-be. The average number of kittens in a litter is four, but Siamese cats tend to have larger litters than other breeds.

Constricted pupils indicate she is relaxed

The unborn kitten

If you suspect your cat is pregnant, you can confirm the pregnancy by checking whether the nipples are pink and the belly is increasing in size. Between four to five weeks after conception you should be able to feel golf-ball-sized swellings. Prodding or poking can damage the embryo or even induce a miscarriage, so any manual examination should be gentle. Your cat should also start to behave maternally. The pregnancy lasts for nine weeks. Halfway through gestation, the embryo is already a perfectly formed miniature kitten. It then develops rapidly, weighing around 3½ ounces (100 grams) at birth.

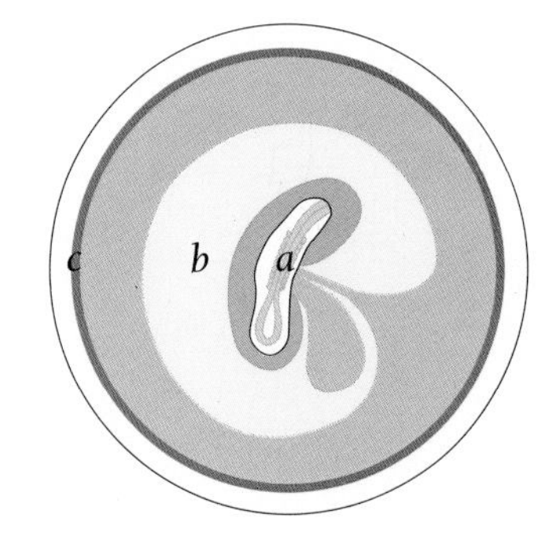

Sixteen days
The embryo (a) is surrounded by fluid (b) and is attached to the wall of the uterus (c).

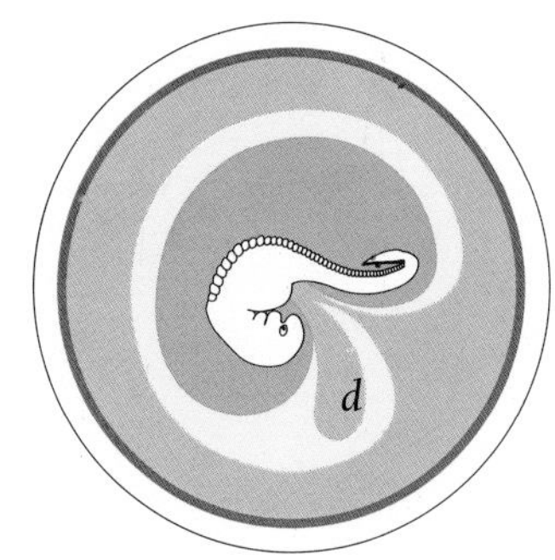

Eighteen days
Head, backbone and tail are obvious. The embryo feeds off nutrients in the yolk sac (d).

Behaving maternally

Even before your cat starts gaining weight and looking obviously pregnant, her appetite will increase and she will become less active. Closer to term, she will groom herself more frequently, especially her abdomen and genital areas. As birth approaches she will spend more time in her chosen nest, impregnating it with her scent. This will help her soon-to-be-born kittens in their orientation towards home.

> *I just don't seem to be able to get comfortable.*

Leg stretches out to find a relaxed position

Nipples are pink and obvious, in preparation for suckling

Preserving strength

(ABOVE) To conserve the energy she will need to give birth, the expectant mother becomes less active. She tends to sit and lie down more of the time. An increase in the level of progesterone, the pregnancy hormone, causes this relaxed, maternal behavior.

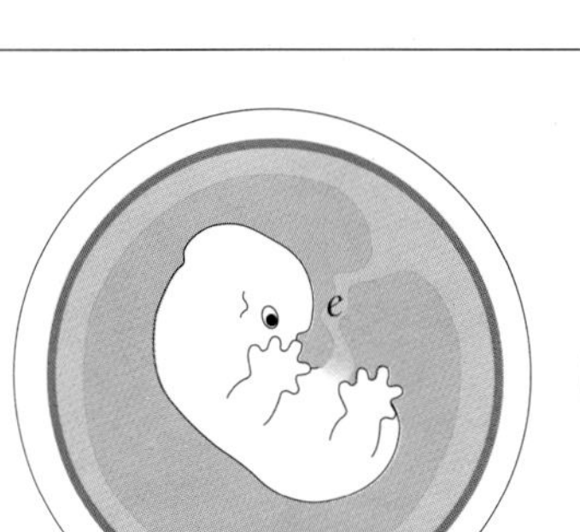

Twenty-one days

The limbs are visibly forming, as are the eyes. Food comes via the umbilical cord (e).

Twenty-eight days

All the internal organs have developed. The tiny kitten is about 1in (2.5cm) long.

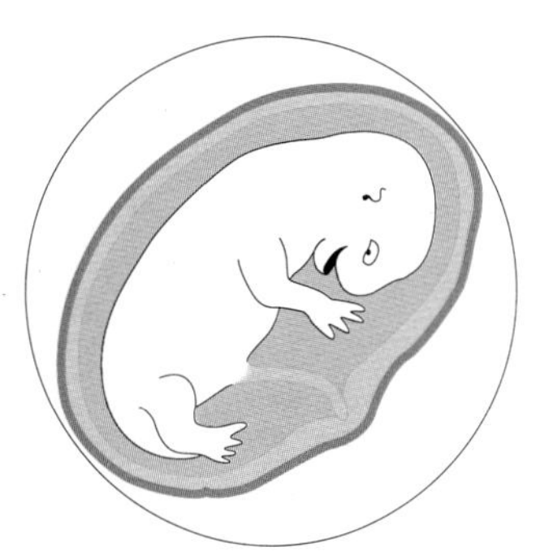

Thirty-five days

The developing fetus grows rapidly and is now about 2½in (6cm) long.

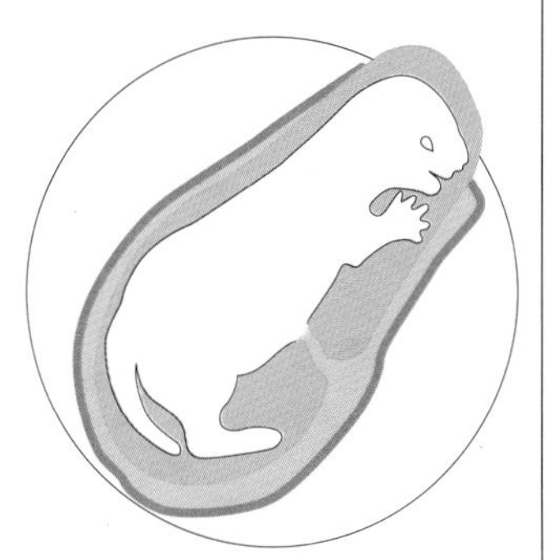

Sixty-three days

The kitten is ready to emerge. In the last 28 days it has doubled in length.

Giving Birth

THE BIRTH IS seldom very difficult. Any time between 60 and 70 days after mating, the mother's biological clock alters her hormone production and labor begins. She will seek out the site chosen for the birth – a secluded, warm place with a surface she can dig at. Her breathing quickens and she might start to purr rhythmically. As labor continues, she will usually produce a vaginal discharge, and soon after will begin to strain. Once the contractions are occurring about every 30 seconds, a delivery is imminent. A resourceful and healthy mother will usually manage her birth without your help.

Don't fuss. I can manage on my own.

Rear leg held high out of the way

1 Labor begins *The kitten emerges from the birth canal in a lubricated sac. The mother has good control of her abdominal muscles, and she concentrates on pressing down to get the kitten out. Her leg lifts up out of the way.*

Relaxed leg indicates easing of contractions

2 The birth *The kitten is born and the labor pains ease, allowing the mother to bend to reach the amniotic sac and lick it away. Licking is an instinctive response. The kitten is being born in a "diving" head-and-feet first position; about 70 percent of kittens are born facing this way.*

Tongue peels away sturdy membrane

Each kitten emerges in its own amniotic sac

3 Cleaning up
(RIGHT) The mother tidies the area around the newborn kitten, eating the amniotic sac. The kitten is helpless, and she licks her dry to prevent her from getting cold. At this point she is still attached by the umbilical cord.

4 The lick of life
(BELOW) The mother now licks the kitten's face to clear all the mucus from her nostrils and mouth. She is naturally vigorous and quite rough – the licking action must make the kitten gasp. The kitten's lungs will then inflate, and she will start to breathe freely.

5 Hiding the evidence
After the birth of each kitten, the mother prepares herself for the next. She licks all the fetal fluids from her belly, around her genital area and even from the floor. For the time being she disregards those kittens that have been born.

After Delivery

1 Two jobs at once *(LEFT) Lapsing in concentration, the mother licks one kitten while giving birth to another. Soon she will attend to the newborn, licking the membrane away. The more litters a cat has produced, the more competent she will be in the birth process.*

> *My babies rely on me for everything.*

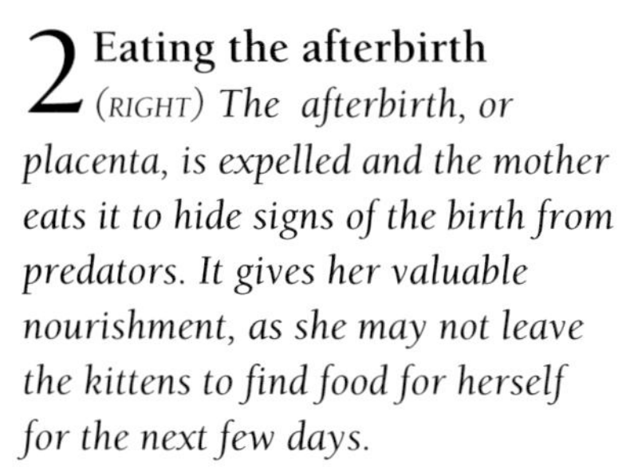

2 Eating the afterbirth
(RIGHT) The afterbirth, or placenta, is expelled and the mother eats it to hide signs of the birth from predators. It gives her valuable nourishment, as she may not leave the kittens to find food for herself for the next few days.

Mother eats nutrient-rich afterbirth for sustenance

3 Severing the cord
(BELOW) The mother cat chews off the umbilical cord about 1 in (2.5 cm) away from the kitten. With her head at an angle, she uses her side, or carnassial, teeth in a shearing action. An inexperienced mother may need help with this. The mother then cleans up all the bloody discharge.

4 Preparing the meal
(BELOW) Sometimes, even before the last kitten has been delivered, the mother curls into a horseshoe shape, drawing her kittens toward her nipples with her paw. The kittens paddle toward the feeding station and nuzzle in to feed at the exposed nipples.

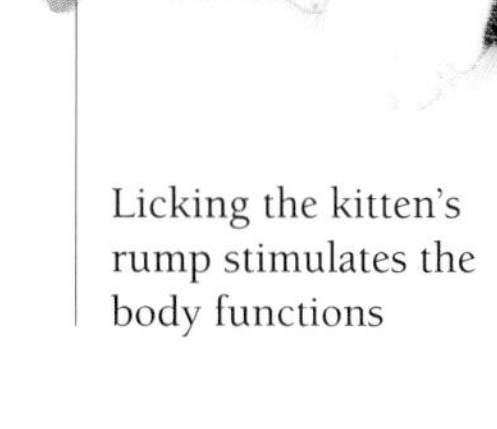

Licking the kitten's rump stimulates the body functions

Survival

The survival of the litter depends upon the mother's ability to stimulate their breathing and keep them warm. She must also feed all of them and protect them from danger. To hide the signs of the helpless newborn, she licks away all birth fluids and eats the afterbirths.

Caring for the Newborn

THE INTERVAL BETWEEN births can be as little as five minutes or as long as two hours. With very large litters, the mother may deliver only some of the kittens, and settle down, exhausted, to feed them. She will then go into labor once more, up to 24 hours later, to give birth to the remainder of the litter. Newborn kittens are helpless and rely on their mother to provide food, protection and warmth. She is instinctively maternal and will start to lick and feed them as soon as they are born, rarely leaving them during their first 48 hours of life.

The lonesome kitten
(ABOVE) *Huddled against his mother for warmth and security, this single kitten is at a disadvantage because he is denied the social development of growing up in a large litter.*

Location of heat receptors, the kitten's most developed capacity

Kittens snuggle together for warmth

Pink feet indicate that circulation is working well

Sibling rivalry
In a large litter there is competition between the kittens. The rivalry is healthy as it produces a creative environment. However, sometimes a loser, or "runt," emerges.

I'm completely exhausted, but I must look after my kittens.

Undivided attention

The mother cat responds to her kittens' cries by licking them as they burrow in for a meal. The last kittens to be born are still damp, but her licking has stimulated their breathing. Their circulation is now also working well – this can be seen by the pink feet and bellies.

Do not disturb

(ABOVE) *The mother will be irritated if you disturb her, and may hiss and spit. Staying close to her kittens, she pants with exhaustion. Soon she will relax and settle down to feed them.*

Protecting the Kittens

THE MOTHER BONDS quickly with her newborn, and instinctively knows how to care for them. Even a first-time mother responds to her kittens' cries by retrieving them when they wander away from her. She is able to recognize each kitten in her litter by its distinctive smell, secreted from skin glands on the head. Kittens rest only when they are huddled with their mother or with each other. Just when they appear to be accustomed to their new environment, the mother abandons the soiled nest and moves them to a safer site. This behavior stems from living in the wild, where it is necessary to move away from any signs of the birth, which might encourage dangerous predators.

Defenseless at birth
The newborn kitten is unable to see, hear or walk. She uses heat receptors on her face to seek her mother out.

Delicate mouthful
The mother moves from the soiled nest when her kittens are four days old. She carries one at a time, grasping each one in her jaws, while the kitten remains relaxed and passive.

Wide-jawed grasp carries kitten safely

"I don't think we're safe here – let's move on."

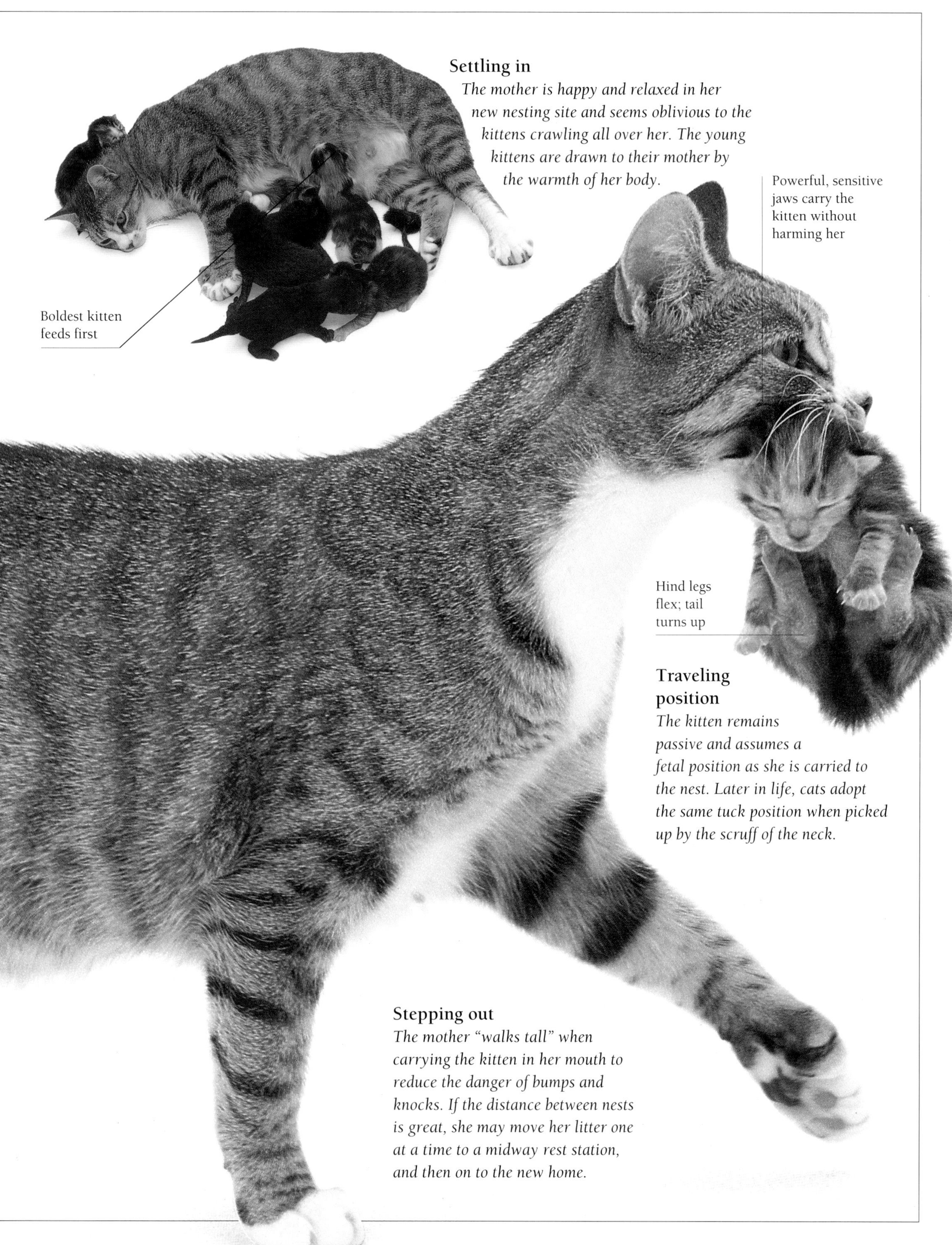

Settling in

The mother is happy and relaxed in her new nesting site and seems oblivious to the kittens crawling all over her. The young kittens are drawn to their mother by the warmth of her body.

Traveling position

The kitten remains passive and assumes a fetal position as she is carried to the nest. Later in life, cats adopt the same tuck position when picked up by the scruff of the neck.

Stepping out

The mother "walks tall" when carrying the kitten in her mouth to reduce the danger of bumps and knocks. If the distance between nests is great, she may move her litter one at a time to a midway rest station, and then on to the new home.

Nursing

Eyes open
The kitten, now six days old, has opened his eyes. Although controlled genetically, kittens reared by young mothers or in dark dens open their eyes earlier than normal.

1 Milk station
(BELOW) Nipples toward the rear of the mother have the most abundant milk supply. They are claimed by the more dominant kittens, who usually grow to be strong and secure.

MOTHERS ARE VERY calm when feeding their kittens, an influence of the pregnancy hormone progesterone. This hormone stimulates milk production and gives the mother a voracious appetite. The first milk that she produces, the colostrum, protects the kittens from many diseases. During the first days the kittens' senses develop rapidly. They learn the scent of their favorite nipple and quickly develop a preference for it. Usurpers often give up sucking when an owner claims his preferred nipple.

Come on, there's room for you all.

Total relaxation
The hormone progesterone, which causes the milk to flow, leaves the mother contented. The constricted pupils indicate that her state of arousal is low.

2 Jockeying for position

(RIGHT) *For the first few weeks the kittens are totally dependent on their mother to position herself so that they can suckle. The runt is unwittingly kept from feeding by the mother. She stretches out her paw and the runt is rejected.*

Sleep position assumed for suckling

Less dominant kitten may develop into a runt

Mother pushes kittens towards her nipples

Kittens paddle toward nipples with hindpaws

3 Drinking time

(BELOW) *There is a limit to the amount of time the kittens are allowed to feed. The mother starts to get up, forcing the kittens to release their grasp. The kitten that has not managed to suckle wanders off. Though the mother is watchful, she will show concern only if she hears a distress call.*

Most productive nipples are in abdominal region

Feeding over, the kitten lifts her head and lets go

This kitten has given up and is wandering off

Fostering

I'm not worried that these kittens aren't all mine – they'll all be cared for.

FOSTERING IS NOT a by-product of human intervention in cat breeding. It is a natural feline behavior that evolved to allow some mother cats to leave the den to hunt while others took over the nursing. For several days after birth, the cat's mothering instinct is so powerful that she readily fosters needy orphaned kittens, especially when they are only a few days old. The very young kittens do not discriminate, and willingly take comfort and nourishment from any available female.

Kitten struggles to latch firmly onto a nipple

Two foster kittens suckle the best nipples

The foster mother
This Burmese feeds her own Tonkinese kittens as well as the two Seal point Siamese that were introduced to the family when they were only a few days old. The foster kittens have settled in well, and are competing with the mother's kittens for food.

The family unit
The kittens are a close-knit group, just like a normal litter, huddling together in the security and warmth of physical contact. Growing up as a foursome will mean more opportunity for play and their mental abilities will mature faster.

Plenty for everyone
The Tonkinese kitten has now found a nipple, which she will defend for herself. Her mother continues to feed all the kittens until it is time for weaning. Fostering usually prolongs milk production as the additional suckling stimulates milk flow.

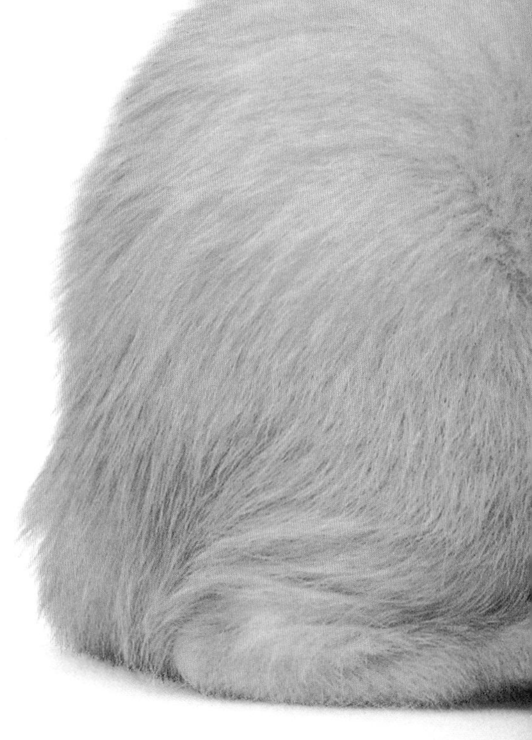

Hand feeding
Even when a kitten is hand-fed from a rubber dropper he will knead with his paws for comfort. He presses on the towel in the same way that he would normally knead the mammary tissue of his mother. This action stimulates milk flow.

Hand rearing

You can hand feed an orphaned kitten on specially prepared milk replacement, using a dropper. The kitten will receive satisfactory nourishment, but unless he is brought up with other cats he will lack vital social contact from other kittens and his nursing mother. This can result in emotional deprivation, and the kitten may not develop a cat's social graces. When an adult he is likely to be a poor breeder.

Kindergarten kittens

Collective upbringing is most common in groups of feral city cats. A contingent of nursing mothers can jointly care for as many as 40 kittens. This form of raising provides intense social activity for the kittens. However, competition for a teat is great, and so smaller kittens are often disadvantaged.

Seal point Siamese have darkened "points" on the ears

The Growing Kitten

Breaking away
This kitten is just starting to investigate life away from mother.

Within a few weeks of birth, your kitten will evolve from total dependence upon mother and siblings to a state of complete independence. At three weeks of age, he will begin to explore and play with the rest of the litter and his mother. The senses of sight, hearing, taste, smell and touch are fully developed by the time he is five weeks old, and by 12 weeks he will have the agility, mobility and all the graces of the adult cat.

Feeling curious
As he develops, a kitten will learn more about his environment.

Under normal circumstances, play increasingly ends in squabbles within the litter. The more dominant kittens convert play into displays of superiority, and what was previously joyful, uninhibited activity now becomes a more serious show of strength. Play between males and females is less frequent as

Secure base
When frightened, kittens still run back to mother for comfort.

Making friends
Firm friends at an early age, kitten and squirrel are going to be friends for life.

the litter becomes more sexually mature. When kittens are raised in our homes, we guarantee them security, warmth, comfort and food. This obviously reduces any need for them to develop into the self-sufficient hunters they need to become to survive in the wild. Self-domesticated by choice, the cat has evolved a pattern of behavior appropriate to the less challenging environment of our homes.

We often interrupt the cat's natural sexual cycle by neutering kittens before they reach puberty. This alters natural odors and reduces many of the tensions inherent in one kitten's relations with another. Therefore, pet cats often have less to fight about, and the kitten's fearless play with siblings can last a lifetime because the struggles over dominance and territory are no longer of paramount importance.

Becoming agile
The successful hunter must be able to leap and pounce. By 12 weeks the kitten will have developed the full range of adult movements.

Power games
Ear positions and bite attempts indicate that, in this instance, play has become a serious dispute over issues of dominance.

Developing the Senses

SERIOUS LEARNING begins at three weeks of age when all the kitten's sensory abilities are coming alive. In order to be successful hunters, kittens have to develop a sense of smell and taste; they need to be vocal to express their feelings, and they must be agile and learn to move confidently.

Distress call

(LEFT) *With mouth wide open, this anxious kitten cries for her mother. The voice is functional from birth, and the kitten uses her voice box to make the distress cry when hungry, trapped, cold or isolated from her mother or siblings. To us, the sound is similar to that made by a human baby. Mothers soon learn to distinguish the cry of their own kittens from others.*

What's going on here? I'm curious – I want to find out more.

Heads down and sniffing

Curiosity develops early. These kittens are using their sense of smell to explore their surroundings. Smell is the first sense to develop completely and is the most developed at birth.

Tail is large in relation to rest of body to assist with balance

Fluid in the eye is cloudy until five weeks of age

Placement of the paw is still a little haphazard

A sense of balance

(ABOVE) *The three-week-old kitten has just mastered walking. Still learning to balance, he is rather clumsy. Tentatively picking up one paw at a time, he makes steps with widely placed feet. Although the touch receptors on the paws are developed, the brain cannot fully understand the stimuli.*

Relying on Mother

CURIOSITY DEVELOPS in kittens much earlier than fear, and once they can walk they will totter off to investigate any new sight, sound or smell. Although they quickly become gregarious, outgoing and inquisitive, young kittens remain overwhelmingly dependent on their mother for feeding, cleaning and rescuing from danger. It is left to her to observe her kittens' activities and to retrieve them when she thinks they may be at risk. Until about the age of six weeks she is their source of nourishment, providing them with the necessary contact for full physical and emotional development.

Vigilant mother
The mother always keeps a watchful eye on her litter. Here, she retrieves a kitten that has strayed too far. As the kitten grows, the skin becomes looser and the neck grasp is more difficult.

Sanitation service
For the first three weeks, the mother stimulates her kittens to urinate and defecate by licking their anogenital regions. She consumes all their bodily discharges. Once they move on to solid food she becomes less inclined to be their sanitation unit.

First steps
This precocious four-week-old kitten is already venturing out on his own. The mother stands by, observing her kitten's progress.

I know you're always there to get me out of trouble.

Creature comforts

(ABOVE) *This seven-week-old kitten still thrives on physical contact with her mother. The mother cat's facial expression shows that she is slightly annoyed at being used as a climbing frame, but she offers no resistance.*

Food and security

At six weeks the kittens no longer depend on their mother's milk for nourishment, but they still continue suckling. With their heads close together, the kittens compete with each other for a nipple. They enjoy the security of being with their mother as she relaxes, cleaning the rump of one of them. Weaning kittens earlier than six weeks will restrict their normal emotional development.

Stepping Out

KITTENS CAN CRAWL from birth. Heat receptors on the nose tell them where to find their mother. At two weeks the brain is receiving information from the other senses to help develop fluid movement. At seven weeks the kitten moves like an adult, and by ten weeks he will be able to walk along narrow ledges, such as the top of a fence, balancing perfectly.

> *Let's get going.*

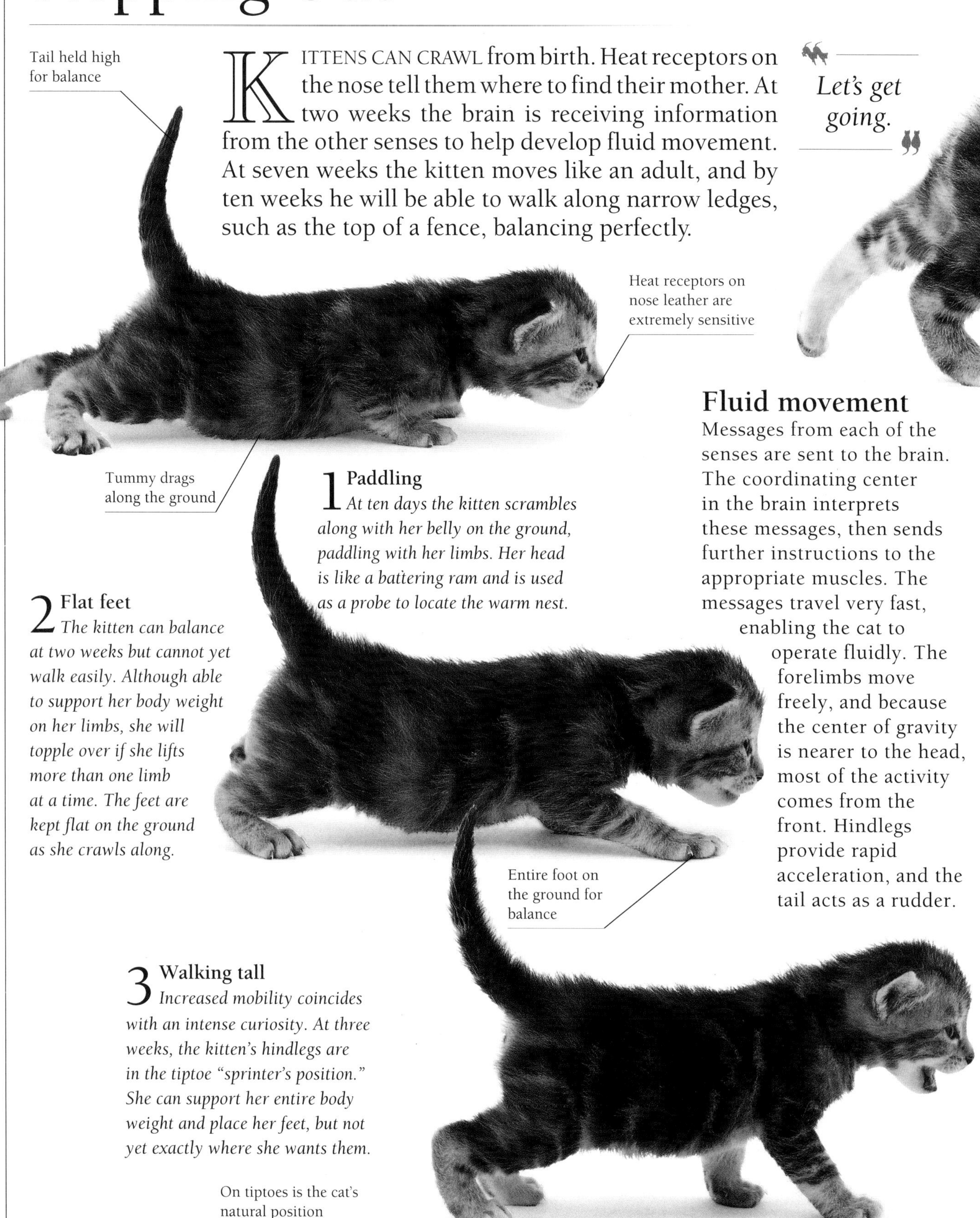

Fluid movement

Messages from each of the senses are sent to the brain. The coordinating center in the brain interprets these messages, then sends further instructions to the appropriate muscles. The messages travel very fast, enabling the cat to operate fluidly. The forelimbs move freely, and because the center of gravity is nearer to the head, most of the activity comes from the front. Hindlegs provide rapid acceleration, and the tail acts as a rudder.

1 Paddling
At ten days the kitten scrambles along with her belly on the ground, paddling with her limbs. Her head is like a battering ram and is used as a probe to locate the warm nest.

2 Flat feet
The kitten can balance at two weeks but cannot yet walk easily. Although able to support her body weight on her limbs, she will topple over if she lifts more than one limb at a time. The feet are kept flat on the ground as she crawls along.

3 Walking tall
Increased mobility coincides with an intense curiosity. At three weeks, the kitten's hindlegs are in the tiptoe "sprinter's position." She can support her entire body weight and place her feet, but not yet exactly where she wants them.

Homing instinct

Once on the move, cats seem to have the ability to find their way back home. Trials have shown that cats use the earth's magnetic field for navigation: cats put in a maze emerged in the direction of home; those fitted with magnets lost their way. Older cats fared better than younger ones, and all performed better when less than 8 miles (12 kilometers) from home.

4 Confidence building *The kitten still has to concentrate hard on where to place her feet, but she is unlikely to topple over at four weeks of age. The organ of balance in the ear is developed enough for stalking and chasing siblings and other objects.*

5 The small adult *When five weeks old, the kitten moves fluently. She does not need to concentrate so intently and is able to move naturally, mimicking her mother. The tail drops as it is no longer needed as a rudder.*

6 Complete agility *The kitten has learned all the movements necessary for survival by the time she reaches ten weeks. She is able to stride confidently along a branch, with no danger of falling. Although still small, she now has all the characteristics of a fast, agile and silent hunter.*

Leaps and Bounds

DESIGNED TO BECOME hunters, kittens rapidly develop an enviably fluid and graceful agility. This enables them to alter the position of their bodies and catch unsuspecting prey at a moment's notice. At six weeks their sense of balance is better than a human's will ever be. This is because a large part of the cat's brain is devoted to receiving and interpreting messages from the organ of balance and from the eyes. The skeleton – particularly the backbone and joints – and muscles are well adapted for pouncing, climbing and balancing.

Impromptu jump
Springing spontaneously into the air, the kitten twists at the waist to face the prey, bending her body into a U-shape. One foot is kept on the ground for balance. Extremely strong ligaments around the joints add extra thrust to the powerful thigh muscles.

One paw remains on the ground for stability

Tail drops as forepaws are raised

Ready to pounce
The kitten creeps up on her prey and then, keeping her hindlegs on the ground, springs forward to catch it unawares. The pounce is the hunting maneuver most frequently used by a cat.

Powerful leg muscles allow full height to be reached

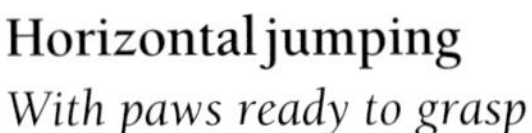

Horizontal jumping
With paws ready to grasp the prey, the kitten leaps forward to cover distance, but she may also inadvertently frighten off her victim.

Ears alert as kitten lands

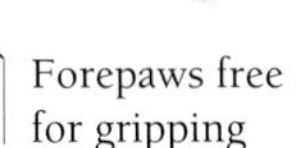

Forepaws free for gripping

Hindpaws land first

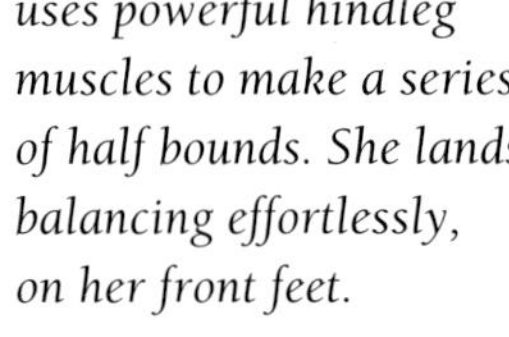

Planned leaping
Calculating to reach a particular point, the kitten uses powerful hindleg muscles to make a series of half bounds. She lands, balancing effortlessly, on her front feet.

Sometimes I think I could fly if I really tried.

Vertical leaping
All four feet lift off the floor as the kitten jumps up and back. Once airborne, the claws unsheathe, ready to grasp on to anything. The leap is used later in life to catch birds and flying insects.

Crash landing
Not every movement is successful, but the kitten's acute righting reflex ensures that she will land upright. The paws are held far apart to help absorb shock. The lack of bony attachments between the forelimbs and the body makes the landing softer and easier.

Landing feet first

Cats spend a lot of time on lookout duty. They choose trees, ledges and rooftops for their observation posts. With all this climbing comes the risk of a fall, so in conjunction with their agility cats have evolved a superb sense of balance. If a cat falls, her body rotates in the air, turning her right way up before she reaches the ground.

Weaning

SOONER OR LATER kittens become a nuisance to their mother. Exactly when this occurs varies from litter to litter. In general, however, kittens are completely weaned at seven weeks, but some mothers get fed up with the razor-sharp teeth much earlier than this. Others may continue to suckle for several more months, regardless of milk flow.

In both instances the need for independence eventually overcomes all kittens, and they relinquish the security of mother to brave the perils and uncertainties of adulthood.

Separation begins
(ABOVE) This six-week-old kitten does not need her mother's milk, but she will stay close by for several more weeks.

Cutting the apron strings
(ABOVE AND BELOW) At six weeks, the kittens in this large litter are still voracious feeders. Their mother becomes less willing to spend time with them as they are a physical drain on her. Their milk teeth, which are very sharp, also cause her discomfort.

Breakfast call

Even though these kittens are of weaning age, the mother takes the initiative and licks them gently awake for breakfast. Maternal care varies from mother to mother, but the kitten's personality is certainly influenced by her behavior.

Suckling for comfort

(BELOW) *With only two kittens in her litter, this mother has found feeding much less of a physical drain than would be the case with a large litter. At seven weeks the milk has almost dried up, but suckling is a comfort behavior that sometimes continues beyond seven weeks.*

I want to keep on suckling for as long as I can.

Forming Friendships

BETWEEN THE AGES OF two and seven weeks, it is essential that your kitten is mentally stimulated if he is to mature into a secure, extroverted cat. Initially, the kitten's social activity centers on his mother and gradually transfers to his siblings. At about two weeks kittens start to play with one another, and this social interaction teaches them how to make friends. This playing gently introduces them to the concerns of adulthood.

"Let's play grown-ups."

Turning "belly-up" is a relaxed response

Mock aggression
These three-week-old kittens are making mock-aggressive rushes at each other, playing rough-and-tumble games. At four weeks they will be wrestling, and at five weeks they will pounce on each other.

Crouched in the basket, the kitten feels secure

Fleeting friendships

Kittens are happy to play with each other until they are 14 weeks old. In fact, play helps keep them together when their mother is absent, hunting for food. They practice aggressive gestures to establish which displays intimidate their siblings most effectively. Some aspects of play, such as biting the nape of the neck, rehearse sexual behavior; others train the kittens to hunt. The kittens will stalk and pounce as if they were preying on each other.

Rough and tumble

Aged three-and-a-half weeks, these kittens roll together and tussle. The sparring may look serious, but at this stage it is for fun. A hugging and licking session will usually follow this kind of play fight.

Fighting talk

(LEFT) *This six-week-old kitten backs off from the fight. Games that once ended amicably now often conclude with a glower and a hiss.*

Creative play

(LEFT) *The kittens are relaxed as one turns onto her side to expose her tummy. Her sister plays with her tail, learning that she must react quickly to catch moving objects.*

Playful attack

The mother engages in playful advances from one six-week-old kitten while another suckles. As her kittens mature, she will become increasingly intolerant of their antics. Other adult cats seldom respond with aggression, but may swat or growl if pestered repeatedly.

Making Contact

I've never seen anything quite like that before!

PLAY MIGHT APPEAR purposeless, but nature is seldom frivolous. Each aspect of the kitten's play has significance. Play with toys begins at three weeks, when he paws at movable objects. Soon he will be batting, holding and exploring anything that makes him curious. If introduced to humans at this age, he willingly plays and, when older, he will be happy to be part of the family. Both types of play are a means of preparing the kitten for the adult world.

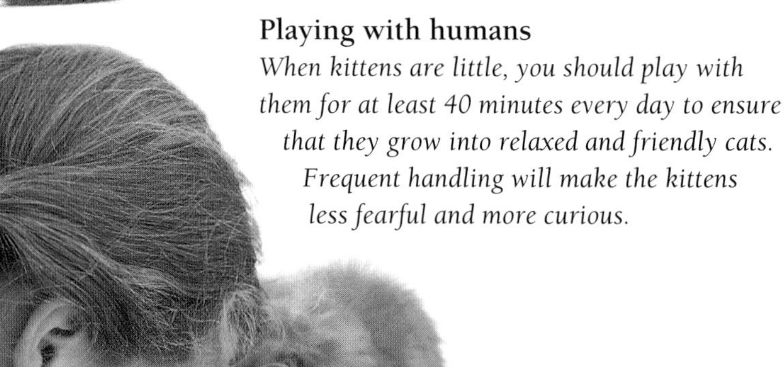

Playing with humans
When kittens are little, you should play with them for at least 40 minutes every day to ensure that they grow into relaxed and friendly cats. Frequent handling will make the kittens less fearful and more curious.

Learning to play ball
(BELOW) *Small balls are favorite toys as they appear to run away. At eight weeks the kitten has full control over the use of his paws and clasps the ball tightly. Like a small child, he is not prepared to share the toy with his sibling.*

Eyes trained on position of ball

Claws retract to hold ball tightly

Moving targets
The kittens watch the ball intently to see if it moves. The ginger kitten touches it inquisitively. The ball rolls away and he chases it, just as he will stalk prey in later life. Learning that the ball rolls silently is as important as learning that breaking a twig makes a noise.

Object play

In playing with different objects such as leaves, or toys such as small balls, kittens learn about their environment. If they are to hunt prey successfully, they must be aware of how things move, react or make a noise when touched. The brain and connections between brain cells develop more in young kittens allowed to play than in kittens deprived of object play.

Ears perk forward to funnel in sounds

Attention focused on sibling

Kitten stares at the ball

Hunting skills
The tabby focuses his attention on the ball. Such staying power suggests that he will develop into a good hunter. The ginger kitten's concentration has wandered from the ball, and he now watches his sibling.

Competing for Position

SOON AFTER THEIR eyes open, kittens begin to tussle competitively with each other. At first the rivalry is playful, but the clumsy paw-blows herald the more serious "ranking" disputes of later life. Eventually, the kitten that is most quick-witted, strongest or most outgoing becomes dominant.

I'm the boss.

Tail fur on end

Sitting on hind-paws gives superior position

Fixed stare unnerves rival

1 Dominant stare (LEFT) *All the play moves are identical to those of hunting or fighting. This kitten stares confidently at her sibling, just as she will later stare at prey. She will stay as still as a statue, hiding any intent, until finally one kitten forces the other to make a move.*

2 Play attack *The kitten standing up is still acting dominantly and, judging by the erect fur on her tail, she is more serious about the game than her sibling, who continues to play. With no fear, the kitten on the ground rolls over to expose her tummy. In this instance, "belly-up-ing" is a typical sign of submission.*

Stalking circle
(RIGHT) *These kittens circle, trying to sniff each other's anal regions. This is a classic rehearsal of the challenges over territory and rank that occur later in life. Cats that know each other sniff noses.*

Developing a hierarchy

At first it would appear that the litter lives together without friction and with equal rights. When the dinner bell rings, all the kittens gather around their mother with no regard as to who should eat first. Ranking in the litter is not as pronounced as it is in a litter of pups, but a hierarchy does develop. In a game the role of dominant kitten may be freely exchanged, but kittens soon learn that they are able to dominate others, or, conversely, that submission is the most practical response to a sibling who is playing more seriously.

3 Escape route
Suddenly the kitten that was playing realizes that her sibling is serious. The game has evolved into a hierarchy dispute and, with ears pinned back in fear, she retreats. Although the other kitten is lying down, the ear position indicates that she has won the challenge.

Enter the Hunter

SOME BEHAVIORISTS BELIEVE that play behavior and hunting are manifestations of the same instinct. This does not explain why your cat will hunt for food and still continue to play like a kitten. Hunting behavior is developed by the time a kitten is five weeks old. At that age kittens use three different hunting maneuvers – the "mouse pounce," the "bird swat" and the "fish scoop" – and it is not long before they learn that there is action in the air as well as on the ground. Most kittens become excellent mousers but, due to relatively poor cat camouflage in many gardens, few will mature into expert bird catchers, so their effect on bird populations would appear to be negligible.

Tail twitches in anticipation

Flexible spine allows unexpected movement

Stalking

(ABOVE) *Stealthily creeping up on her prey, this nine-week-old hunter has mastered the technique of squirming slowly forward. Kittens start stalking each other when they are only three weeks old, and begin to stalk objects a short time later.*

"You won't be able to escape me!"

Mouse pounce

(RIGHT) *The stiff-legged sideways leap is a favorite maneuver of the nine-week-old kitten, practiced here on a button. She springs down on to her "victim" rather than jumping up. Later in her life she may use the mouse pounce to catch rodents.*

Feet firmly planted

Fish scoop

(LEFT) *Practicing on a ball of wool, this kitten learns how to make the flipping action that can be used to scoop a fish out of the water. Claws unleashed in readiness, she throws her paw over her shoulder. The kitten does not need her mother to teach her this gesture as it is instinctive.*

Bird swat

This kitten is still too young at six weeks to do a proper bird swat, but with claws out ready to grasp, she extends her paw to reach up at the unexpected movement in the air. When she is older she will be able to leap into the air from a standing position to swipe at moths, flies and birds that catch her attention.

Balance for hunting

At six weeks this kitten has sufficient balance to free both forepaws to bat airborne objects, but as yet she lacks the muscle coordination to leap successfully. Her tail sticks out straight behind her to help with stability.

Bringing back the spoils

Once captured, prey must be carried away, even if it is only a ball of wool. This kitten brings her toy duck back to the den just as her mother will bring back mice for her kittens.

Breaking Down Boundaries

From the age of two weeks a kitten can also start to form relationships with prey (squirrel), predator (dog) or competitor (fox). Provided the kitten is able to play with and head- and flank-rub the stranger without being frightened away, it does not seem to matter where an animal fits in the cat hierarchy. Such friendships can be lifelong, but the period during which these bonds may form is short-lived, lasting for a maximum of five weeks.

Befriending the enemy
(LEFT) *Showing no fear, this kitten clambers up onto the dog to seek out warmth and security. Gentle adult dogs or puppies less than 12 weeks old are ideal for these early social meetings.*

Exploring the differences
(BELOW) *This kitten enjoys a relaxed relationship with the fox cub. Until he is seven weeks old, the kitten looks upon different species simply as other kittens or as cats that either smell or look different.*

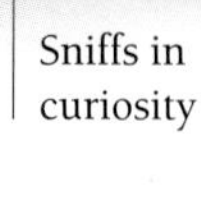

Sniffs in curiosity

Critical timing

The permanent fear a cat has of other species, for example a fox or dog, and the instinct to prey on small species such as a mouse or rat, does not develop until after the kitten is seven weeks old. Studies show that when six-week-old kittens are raised with rats they consistently refuse to prey upon that breed of rat later on in life. But if the first meeting is delayed beyond seven weeks, the relationship turns into one of hunter and hunted.

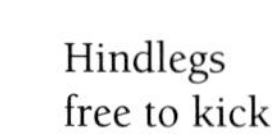

Hindlegs free to kick

Fear of the unknown
Fearful yet inquisitive, this kitten's hackles are partly raised and his back is arched as he investigates the squirrel. There is great curiosity about small species that are the size of prey.

"Hello, friend – let's play."

Hierarchy play
(BELOW) *The kitten and fox cub play a game of dominance and submission in the same way that kittens play together. Here, the kitten is feigning aggression by rolling over to expose teeth and claws.*

Mock attack
(BELOW) *The kitten attacks the squirrel playfully, but he will not "bite home." When older it is unlikely that he will kill squirrels. The squirrel is not frightened as it was raised with cats.*

Learning to Survive

KITTENS ARE TAUGHT how to catch and kill prey by their mother. This is an essential skill for feral cats, but even your pet cat will teach her kittens how to find and hunt for food, despite the fact that you usually provide regular meals in a food bowl. To begin with, the kittens must learn to identify potential victims, so initially the mother brings prey home dead. Next the kittens must learn how to kill, so she returns with live prey.

At first the kittens may be apprehensive and fearful, but they soon become brave enough to chase and capture chosen prey, throwing it before finally making the kill. Kittens raised by a mother that is a successful hunter are more likely to become successful hunters themselves, as a good teacher passes on special skills. However, kittens can still become adept hunters without training from their mother.

Providing prey
(ABOVE) This mother cat has just killed a mouse to bring home for her kittens to play with. Her rigid stance and dilated pupils show her excitement. She will warn them she is returning with prey. They soon learn to interpret the vowel sounds that tell them if she has a mouse, or, much more dangerous, a rat that may fight tenaciously.

Careful examination
Under the watchful eye of their mother, the kittens examine the dead mouse that she has brought home for them. By mimicking their mother's behavior, the kittens learn to use all their senses to investigate the rodent thoroughly. Its scent will become a lifelong memory.

My mother will teach me everything I need to know.

Preparing to eat
(RIGHT) While the mother grooms one of her kittens to distract it, the other kitten concentrates on the mouse, holding it in her forepaws and kicking with her hindlegs.

Playing with prey
Unfamiliar prey stimulates this kitten to play with her quarry rather than simply kill and consume it. The old story that a hungry cat kills more rats is inaccurate because hunger motivates only the most experienced of hunters.

Making demands
This pet cat stands up on her hindpaws and begs for her food. By watching and listening to her mother, the kitten also learns to beg and make the demand call. Through domestication, the feral cat has evolved from independent hunter into scavenger-beggar.

Becoming Independent

IN THE WILD, where kittens do not experience contact with humans, they mature into lone hunters. There is no incentive to continue the group activity that existed when they were kittens. Independence is often asserted dramatically when the mock aggression of early play determines rank order within the litter. By the time the kittens are 14 weeks old the fights are serious, although the combatants rarely suffer any permanent injuries. The bonds of kittenhood are now broken and the litter disbands. Your kitten continues to accept close contact with you because she regards you as a mother substitute, not a litter-mate.

You're competition. Go away!

1 Play fighting
When fully mobile, at about nine weeks, kittens will start to rehearse aggressive displays. With claws extended, the dominant kitten stands up, ready to pounce. Her sibling is lying down, still thinking that the attack is for fun. But it is for real, and the game may degenerate into a serious fight.

Training ground

The fights of independence are final training for the duels in which mature tomcats engage either for territory or for the right to mate with receptive females. It is also practice for females who might later be called upon to protect their litter or their territory. At this stage, female kittens begin to mature sexually, and they are far less tolerant of physical contact with male siblings.

2 Neck bite *(ABOVE) The submissive kitten suddenly realizes her opponent is serious. She leaps up from the prostrate position and launches a counter-attack, trying to sink her teeth into her sibling's neck.*

3 Lull in hostilities *(RIGHT) At the age of nine weeks the kittens may pause and relax during a fight. The kitten that was mauling assumes a less aggressive stance, while her sibling scrutinizes her, anticipating more activity.*

4 Aggression resumes *(RIGHT) The kitten that was initially dominant makes a flying assault on her sibling, who starts to roll over so that she can defend herself from attack with her claws and teeth.*

THE MATURE CAT

Keen eyesight
As the pupils constrict in bright light, the cat is able to look directly into the sun.

WE KNOW THAT cats can see when there is only one-sixth of the amount of light that we need to see, but we are not sure if they see things in exactly the same way as us. We know that their range of hearing is much more extensive than ours, but we do not know what those high-pitched sounds, inaudible to us, really sound like. We know that cats have special taste buds for water, but what do they actually taste?

Varied diet
Many cats enjoy crunchy dry food. Prepared foods are often preferred to natural prey.

Many of the cat's senses are understood by us, although cats use their senses in different ways. Smell, for example, is important for eating, but also for courtship, hunting, territory-marking and even toilet habits. Grooming is important for self-cleaning, but it is also a way of ridding the body of excess heat or reducing tension.

Mutual grooming
The orange cat's gentle grooming of his companion mimics a mother's grooming of her kittens.

Caught cat-napping
This cat might appear sound asleep but he is actually alert to any unusual sights or sounds that may occur around him.

The cat's ability to balance is among the best developed of all mammals. Cats can climb effortlessly, walk tightropes as if they were broad pavements, and, if they do fall, have the ability to right themselves in midflight and land delicately on their feet.

Cats are world-champion sleepers. We know that their sleep patterns are similar to ours, and that like us they probably dream. However, their courtship and mating behavior is completely different, with much caterwauling, shrieking and patient waiting on the part of numerous hopeful males. Old age, however, vividly reflects the same behavior changes that we undergo. Messages simply take longer to get to the brain. Older cats, good companions throughout their lives, have earned and deserve compassionate understanding.

Washing routine
With saliva applied to his paw, this cat grooms his face in a ritualized manner.

Lapping it up
Unlike dogs, cats have almost perfect table manners. These kittens will finish their milk without spilling a drop.

Eating Habits

CATS ARE OPPORTUNIST hunters. In the wild they survive by eating whenever they catch or find a meal. Their feeding habits in our homes, however, are quite different. Typically, a pet cat will choose to eat between 10 and 20 small meals a day, and will continue to feed throughout the day and night. Your pet cat also has a more varied diet than his self-sustaining relatives, and, although hard food is not a natural part of the hunter's diet, many domestic cats actively prefer prepared, crunchy food.

Don't worry, I'll only take as much as I need.

Aid to digestion
(BELOW) *Settling down to eat, this cat adopts a hunched position, with feet drawn back for comfort. The tail is wrapped around the body to prevent it being stepped on, allowing the cat to concentrate on eating.*

Eating in peace
(ABOVE) *To avoid competing with her young kittens, the mother eats separately, removing her food from the bowl. When given a large lump of food, she will slice it into smaller pieces, which she consumes individually.*

Dry morsel
Offered dry food for the first time, this cat stands rather apprehensively to investigate the pieces.

Shearing teeth
Using the razor-sharp carnassial, or side, teeth, the cat slices large lumps of food into small pieces before swallowing. The small front incisors are useful for scraping off tiny pieces of meat or fish.

The cat and the cream
Using mobile tongues, the kittens take four or five laps before each swallow. They are fastidious drinkers, never spilling a drop.

Smelling and Tasting

YOUR CAT HAS twice as many scent receptors in her small nose as you do. She sniffs to pick up information about food, the presence of other cats and potential danger. From smell she can tell whether a tom owns the territory or if a female is in heat. Your cat is drawn to food by smell rather than taste, and will never taste anything without smelling it first. Her taste buds are sensitive, distinguishing between salt, bitter and acid tastes, but she has no taste buds that respond to sweet tastes. Cats that crave chocolate either have been unwittingly trained to do so or are the result of our intervention in breeding.

Cat aphrodisiac

Sniffing the plant catnip stimulates your cat by activating her biochemical pathways. The scent is taken up into the vomeronansal organ. She responds by rolling around on the ground demonstrating her pleasure. This display of excitement is similar to behavior pre- and post-mating. Only about half of all adult cats will sniff, lick or chew catnip.

Eating carefully

Cats are much fussier eaters than dogs. As true carnivores, felines are unwilling to share our diet and they will usually refuse sweet titbits. Cats are attracted to food by its smell, and particularly by the smell of fat in meat. Mouse meat, their natural food, is 40 percent fat.

Once the smell is found to be acceptable, your cat will taste the food. His sensitive palate prefers foods that have high levels of the chemicals nitrogen and sulphur, the constituents of the amino acids that make up meat. Smell memories are stored in the brain and last a lifetime. These memories, together with the sensitive senses of taste and smell, are self-protective, helping to ensure the cat eats healthily.

Grooming tool

Your cat's tongue is long, muscular and flexible. The sand-paper-like hooks are used in grooming. The taste buds, which include receptors sensitive to the taste of water, are located at the tip, sides and back.

Backward-pointing barbs used in grooming and for scraping meat off bones

Memorizing scents
Sniffing in short bursts, this cat smells a clump of grass. The air is drawn into the vomeronasal organ, a special chamber in the roof of the mouth. Used primarily by males to scent females in heat, this chamber is filled with cells that trap the odor. The smell is converted into electrical signals that are transferred to the brain to create smell memories.

Exploring by smell
Initially attracted to a toad by its movement, this cat explores further by smelling it. Most cats enjoy hunting amphibians, and often present them to their owners as gifts. They will eat them only when absolutely necessary.

"If it smells good, it's bound to taste good too."

Reacting dramatically
An unpleasant taste will make a cat salivate profusely in an attempt to dispel the taste as quickly as possible. Medicines may provoke this response in your cat.

Balancing Act

I can't put a paw wrong.

YOUR CAT'S UNCANNY ability to land on his feet, maintaining perfect balance, is directly connected to his acute hearing. Deep in the ear is the vestibular apparatus, which is filled with fluid, tiny floating crystals and millions of sensitive hairs. These instantly orient the cat so that he can turn his body into an upright position. Related to this innate sense of balance is the cat's acute hearing – sharper than either a dog's or a human's. Your cat is able to hear tone so distinctly that he can distinguish between the sound of your car engine and that of an identical size and make of car.

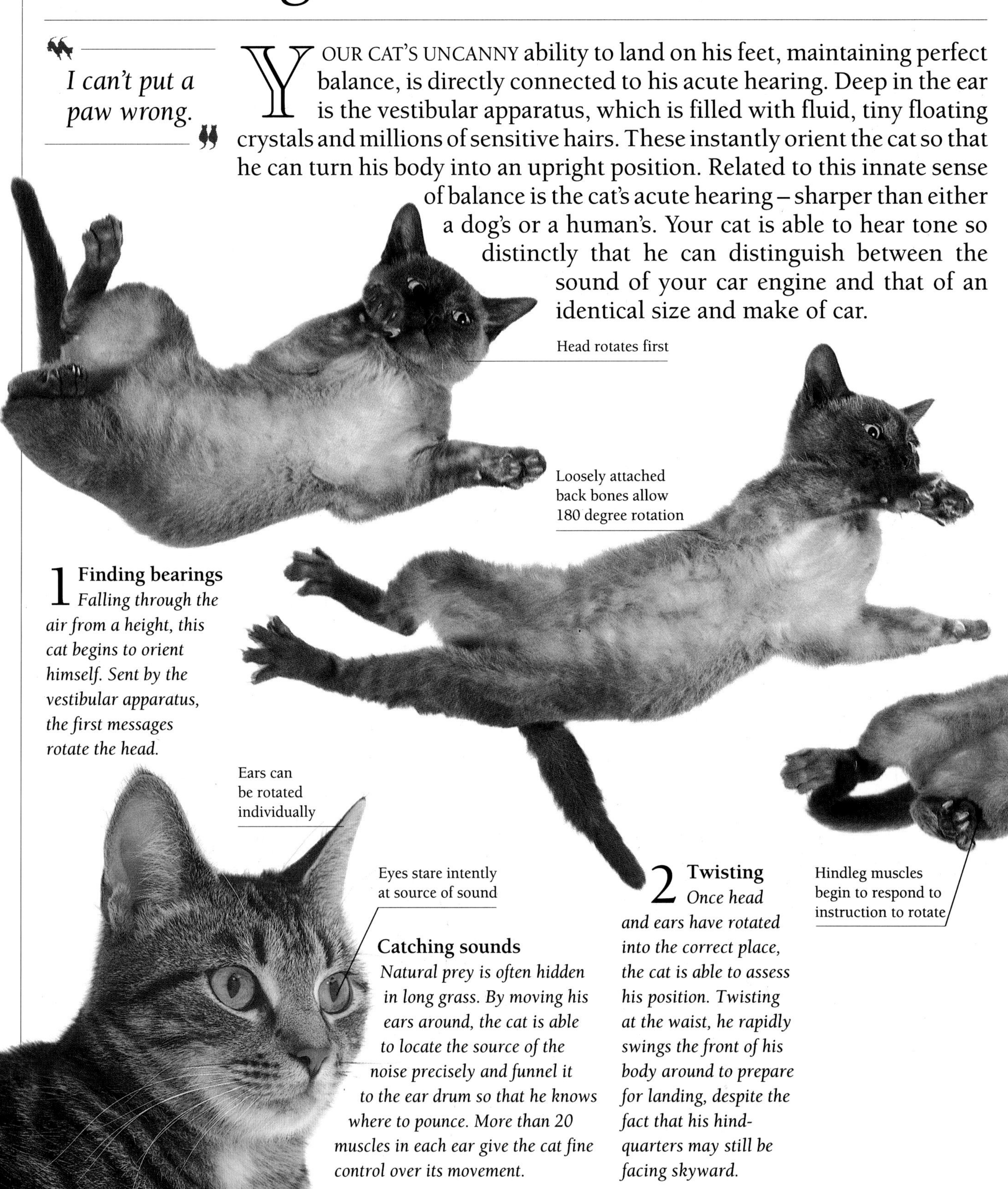

1 Finding bearings *Falling through the air from a height, this cat begins to orient himself. Sent by the vestibular apparatus, the first messages rotate the head.*

Catching sounds *Natural prey is often hidden in long grass. By moving his ears around, the cat is able to locate the source of the noise precisely and funnel it to the ear drum so that he knows where to pounce. More than 20 muscles in each ear give the cat fine control over its movement.*

2 Twisting *Once head and ears have rotated into the correct place, the cat is able to assess his position. Twisting at the waist, he rapidly swings the front of his body around to prepare for landing, despite the fact that his hind-quarters may still be facing skyward.*

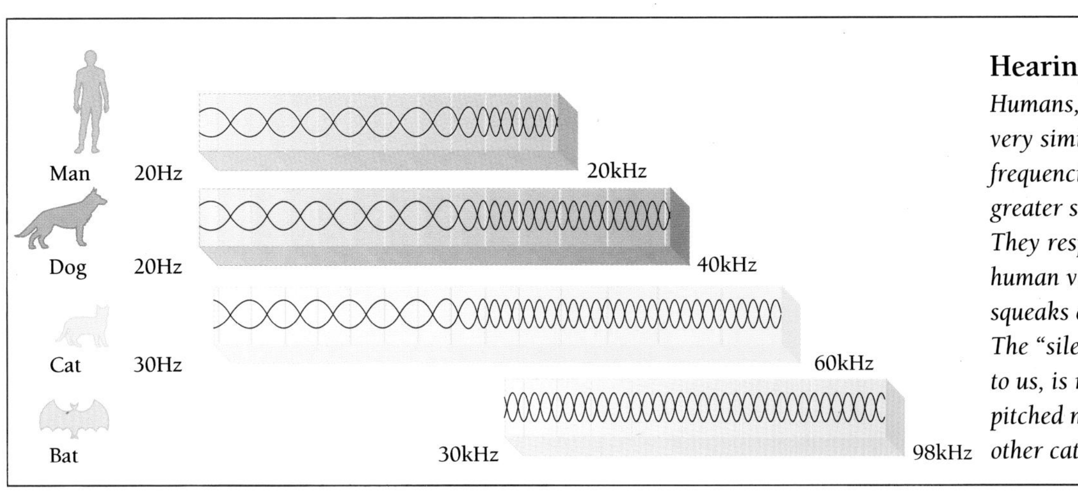

Hearing ranges
Humans, cats and dogs have very similar hearing at low frequencies, but cats have greater sensitivity to high notes. They respond to high-pitched human voices as well as to the squeaks of kittens and mice. The "silent meow," inaudible to us, is really just a high-pitched meow, quite audible to other cats with normal hearing.

Brilliant hearing

Your cat's hearing range covers over ten octaves and can distinguish between two notes that differ from each other by merely one-tenth of a tone. Cats can judge to within 3in (8cm), with 75 percent accuracy, the source of a sound 1yd (1m) away and can hear high-pitched sounds that are inaudible to us.

Turning a deaf ear
This blue-eyed, white cat is suffering from a genetic deafness. She does not turn her head in the direction of a sound or move her ears to locate the position of a noise. White cats with one blue and one yellow eye are often deaf only on the blue side.

Forelimbs stretch out to make ground contact first

3 Absorbing shock
Nearing the ground, the front legs stretch out. With no bone attachments to the rest of the body, the forelimbs absorb shock to prevent injury. The body continues to twist as orientation messages are sent to the hindquarters.

4 Landing feet first
Now ready to land on his forepaws, the cat looks confidently ahead at the landing pad. All his muscles are relaxed because tense muscles are more likely to tear.

Forelimbs act as shock absorbers

Through Your Cat's Eyes

EYES ARE ONE of your cat's most distinctive and mesmerizing features. Appropriate to such opportunist hunters, cat's eyes are designed to collect the maximum amount of light. The eye's surface, or cornea, is curved, and the lens is very large in comparison to the other dimensions of the eye. In dim light, or when your cat is excited or scared, the pupils dilate; in bright light they can close completely, allowing light to pass through two slits at the top and bottom.

I've got the eyes of a hunter.

Shading from glare
(ABOVE) *With pupils the size of pinpricks, this cat can stare into the sun without damaging her retina. Acting like built-in sunglasses, the muscles in the iris allow the pupil to change shape according to the available light. Almost round in the dark, the pupil becomes oval in brighter light. In intense light the slit pupil closes in the middle, leaving two tiny slits at each end.*

Seeing in the dark
(BELOW) *In the restricted light this cat's pupils dilate to become almost spherical, allowing as much light as possible to enter the eye. Contrary to popular belief, cats cannot see any better than us in the pitch dark, but their eyes can function in very dim conditions. This enables the cat to hunt for prey in the dawn light and at dusk.*

Pupils dilate to become spherical

Glowing eyes
(BELOW) *A cat's eyes shine green or gold as light is reflected from layers of mirror-like cells behind the retina. The cells improve the cat's night vision by reflecting back light.*

CAT VISION

Cats focus on the center of their picture

Edge of picture is blurred

HUMAN VISION

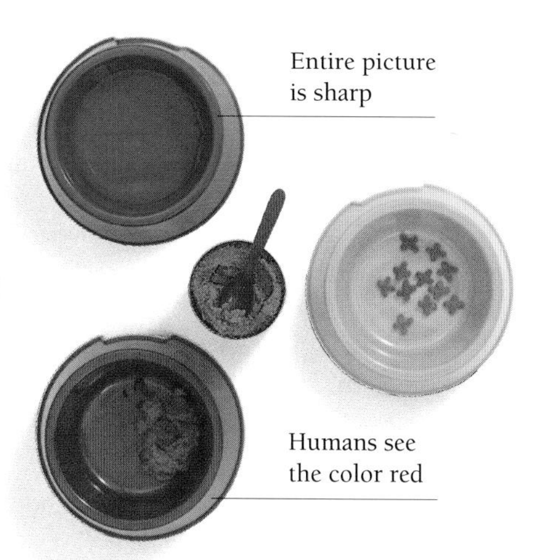

What your cat sees

Cats see green and blue but not red. This is not a significant weakness since smell and taste, rather than color, distinguish prey. Cats focus on the middle of the picture with the periphery remaining slightly cloudy.

The images above demonstrate the differences between what we see (ABOVE LEFT) and what your cat sees (ABOVE RIGHT). He can focus on fast-moving objects clearly because, unlike dogs or humans, his head stays level as he bounds along.

Dilating dramatically

When the "flight-or-fight" response is activated, your cat's pupils dilate. This creates a wider field of vision and actually enables your cat to see more of any potential danger.

Binocular vision

When the two fields of vision overlap, a binocular effect results. Three-dimensional vision is vital to hunting animals, and enables them to judge distances accurately.

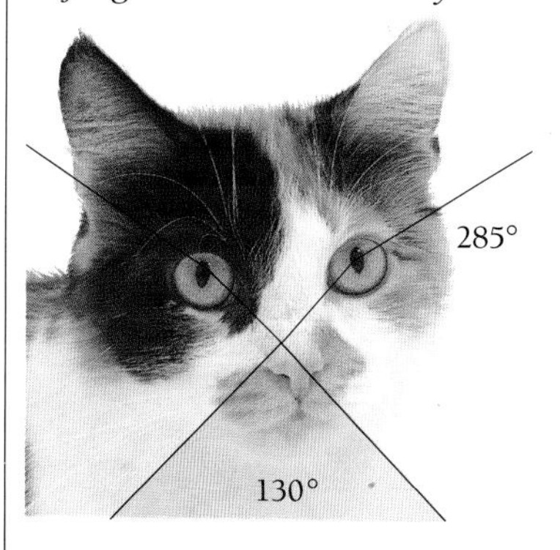

Cat vision

When your cat's eyes face forward, 130 of the total 285 degrees of his field of vision is binocular.

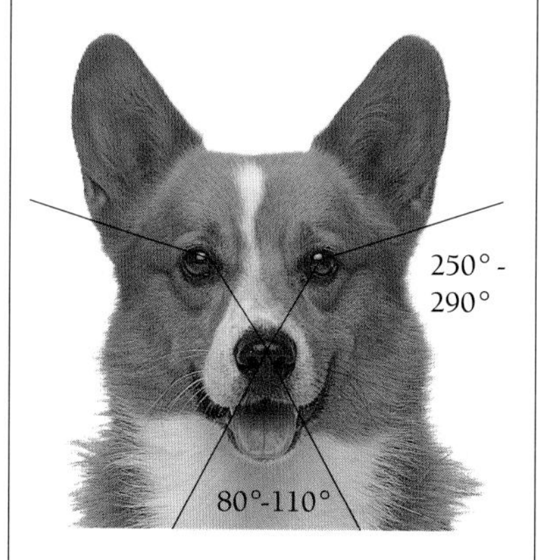

Dog vision

Eyes are set to the side, with up to 110 degrees of binocular overlap.

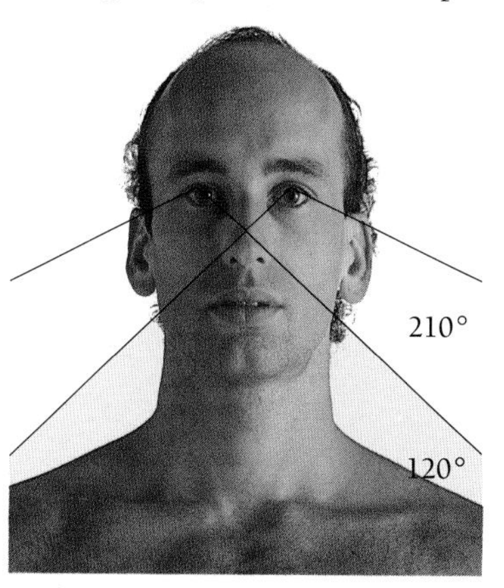

Human vision

Despite a smaller field of vision, our binocular vision is good.

Touching

ALL THE TIME your cat is using her well-developed sense of touch to gather information about her surroundings. The most sophisticated touch receptors are contained in the whiskers which, extending beyond the width of her body, help her to move about confidently. From the information picked up by the whiskers your cat can determine, for example, whether or not she can fit through a narrow gap. Other touch receptors on the body are sensitive to pressure and texture, responding to such things as the sensation of being stroked or the type of surface underfoot. All over your cat's body there are receptors that detect heat and cold. Her preference for the warmth of a fire or radiator may well have come from the ancestors that originated in North Africa.

I know you – so let's rub noses!

Seeking out heat
Cats love heat and are able to withstand much higher temperatures than we can. We start to feel uncomfortable if our skin temperature exceeds 112°F (44°C), but your cat will not feel discomfort until her skin temperature reaches 126°F (52°C).

Touching noses
(RIGHT) *This kitten greets another cat she knows by sniffing his nose. The touch receptors on the nose are already developed at birth and help the kitten find his mother.*

Sensing air currents
Every whisker over your cat's eyes, on her elbows and on her muzzle is rooted in a rich supply of nerve endings. As these specialized antennae-like hairs brush past objects, messages are sent to the brain. Even air currents can be felt, and at night she uses her whiskers to help her pick out a clear path. If she loses her whiskers she may bump into objects when moving around in complete darkness, but the problem is short-lived as new whiskers grow in their place.

Importance of touch

Your cat is more sophisticated than almost any other domestic animal when it comes to using touch to investigate surroundings. Touch may even be the most important sense required for social development. But just as touch is important for learning, *being* touched is even more vital for healthy emotional development. Cats deprived of physical contact become fearful and withdrawn, crouching motionless or perhaps compensating by excessive grooming.

Measuring spaces
Using muzzle whiskers, this cat is able to gauge whether or not she can squeeze her lithe body through the narrow gap in the fence. As her head comes through, she will direct her whiskers to feel the surface below.

Whiskers angled down to detect surface

Receptors on the nose pad explore gently

Basking in comfort
(BELOW) *This kitten enjoys the security of the girl's lap. When he is older, he will not remain in this position or let her tickle his tummy because he will feel too exposed.*

Cat assumes relaxed belly-up position

Grooming

GROOMING IS NOT simply a matter of personal hygiene, it is a reflex behavior. Just as you sometimes scratch your head in thought, your cat may have the urge to groom. Usually your cat will groom herself when she is feeling relaxed, but she may preen if she is frightened. Grooming keeps the fur in pristine condition and, as the saliva evaporates, can also help your cat regulate her temperature.

Total cleansing process
A born contortionist, this cat sticks her leg straight up in the air and then reaches round to clean herself. As she removes matted or soiled fur, the grooming action stimulates the scent-producing anal and perianal glands.

Washing routine
(RIGHT) The routine that your cat follows when she washes her face is always the same. Saliva is applied to the inside of the forepaw, which is rubbed from back to front in a circular motion around the side of her face.

Abrasive tongue combs fur

Clean from top to tail
With her mobile spine, this cat can reach to groom almost every part of her body with her tongue. Turning her head almost 180 degrees, she nibbles away at grit and flakes of dead skin on her back. The order in which she washes her body is random.

Not just a lick and a promise

Your cat is naturally clean. She will instinctively use a specific site as a toilet, and just as fastidiously groom her fur. The licks stimulate the glands in the skin to produce a film of oil that waterproofs her coat. Her hook-covered tongue removes loose and broken hairs and matts, and she uses her tiny front teeth to gnaw at other debris. Long-haired cats may need extra help with grooming. The fine hairs tangle easily and knots often build up in the coat.

Mutual grooming
This kitten licks her mother behind the ears and provides a practical solution to an anatomical problem. With eyes shut tight the mother feels totally relaxed as her kitten grooms her. Mutual grooming also strengthens the intimate bond between mother and offspring.

Keeping clean makes me feel good.

Finishing touches
Applying saliva for a final rinse, she pulls her paw over her eyes to complete the washing cycle. When your cat grooms herself after you have handled her, she may be tasting your scent or, more likely, she may simply be masking your scent with her own.

Head lowered to reach behind the ears

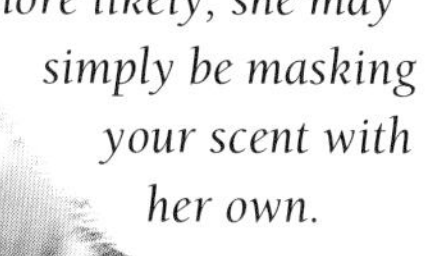

Paw wipes the eyes

Washing behind the ears
Completing the end of a large washing circle, she brings her paw over her ear. Your cat enjoys being stroked on the head because she cannot reach it with her tongue.

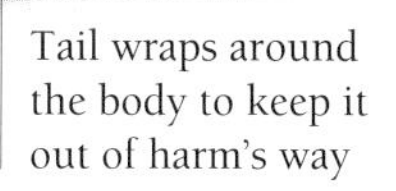

Tail wraps around the body to keep it out of harm's way

Cat Napping

YOUR CAT SPENDS about 16 hours a day sleeping, which is almost twice as long as most other mammals. Exactly why they spend so much time snoozing is not yet understood. They seem to prefer to take their cat naps during the day and are usually active in the early morning and late evening, when hunting is most productive. On waking, they habitually go through a ritual that includes yawning, stretching and grooming.

"Nothing's better than 40 winks."

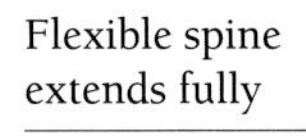

Yawning
Awakening gently, this cat gives a wide yawn to stretch his jaw muscles. Although yawning is a sign of nervousness in other species, it does not appear to be the case with cats.

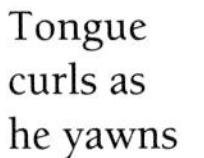

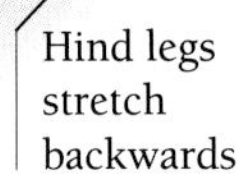

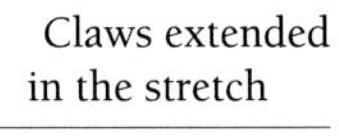

Stretching
After arching her back one way, this cat reaches forward to stretch the muscles in her front legs, claws and neck. Circulation to her extremities is revived and her sense of touch is reawakened.

Tail goes up as she arches her back

Flexing the back
Having woken up slowly, she puts her paws close together and straightens her hindlegs. The elegant arch of her back exercises the muscles. She must keep her finely honed body in peak condition so that she is always ready to produce the short bursts of energy that a hunter requires.

Snoozing in comfort
These young kittens snooze together, enjoying each other's warmth and the security of the basket. As they get older and the social bonds between them break down, they will prefer to sleep alone. They will continue to choose warm, secure spots such as cupboards or your bed for their cat naps.

Waking scratch
As the finale of the stretching ritual, the kitten grooms herself, a habit similar to our morning wash.

Sleeping rhythms

Sleeping is not a passive state. When your cat becomes drowsy, she enters a stage of light sleep from which she is easily aroused. Between ten and thirty minutes later, her whole body becomes slack, her position shifts and she enters a period of deep sleep.

During deep sleep your cat may flex her paws and twitch her whiskers. She almost certainly dreams, and, judging from the amount of electrical activity in the brain, her mind is as active as when she is awake. After around seven minutes of deep sleep she returns to a light sleep. The cycle is then repeated.

Relaxing happily
(RIGHT) *This cat shows no fear of humans because she was raised with them. She happily falls asleep in the girl's arms. The cat looks upon the child as a mother substitute, which is why she enjoys the close physical contact.*

Closed eyes show the cat has no fear

Choosing a Partner

ALTHOUGH ARRANGED MARRIAGES are now the norm for almost all pure-bred cats, when left to nature it is the female prerogative to select her mate. Tomcats might engage in bloody duels for the right to mate with a receptive female, but it is just as likely that she will choose the loser as the father of her litter.

Females normally experience several ten-day cycles of sexual receptiveness each year, which are brought on by increasing daylight in late winter and early spring. Cats housed indoors in artificial light can be sexually active at any time of the year. During her receptive phase, the female undergoes a personality change, becoming affectionate and lascivious.

1 Signalling sexual interest *By rolling provocatively, this female is indicating her availability. She may also tread with her front paws and call out. Even the most withdrawn of females will give these bold signals. Inexperienced cat owners often assume their cat is in distress.*

I'm available.

He advances, avoiding eye contact

2 Tentative approach *While the male advances cautiously, avoiding eye contact and making gentle chirping sounds, the female continues to roll and call repeatedly. He rubs his head against places where she has rolled or rubbed but is careful not to come close to her too quickly. If he does she might turn and swipe at him or run away.*

3 Reducing tension *(ABOVE) Now more confident, the male begins to groom the female behind her ears to relax her and make her less likely to respond aggressively to his advances. Although the female appears passive at this stage, the mating initiative comes completely from her, and it is possible that she will withdraw her invitation at any time.*

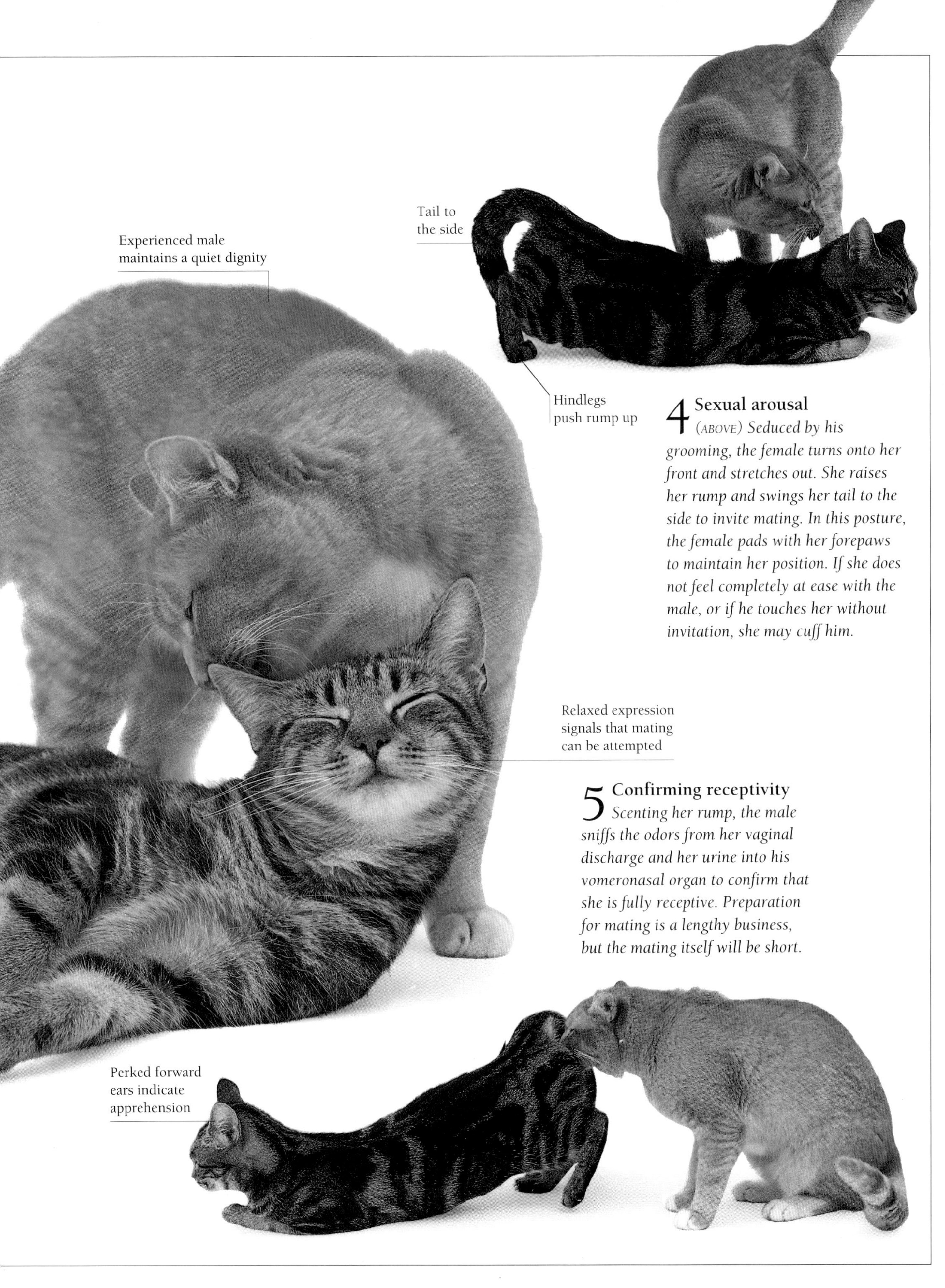

4 Sexual arousal
(ABOVE) Seduced by his grooming, the female turns onto her front and stretches out. She raises her rump and swings her tail to the side to invite mating. In this posture, the female pads with her forepaws to maintain her position. If she does not feel completely at ease with the male, or if he touches her without invitation, she may cuff him.

5 Confirming receptivity
Scenting her rump, the male sniffs the odors from her vaginal discharge and her urine into his vomeronasal organ to confirm that she is fully receptive. Preparation for mating is a lengthy business, but the mating itself will be short.

The Mating Game

CATS DO NOT form pair bonds. When mating ceases, the female has nothing more to do with the male. She is not naturally monogamous, and if several eligible toms are available she might well mate with all of them. Unlike most other domestic animals, cats are induced ovulators, which means that the act of mating stimulates the hormone changes that trigger the release of eggs. Therefore the more frequent the mating, the more likely it is that eggs will be fertilized.

6 Getting into position
With her ears back, the female appears fearful as mating begins. The male starts to mount carefully, opening his mouth wide, ready to grasp the back of her neck should she decide to try to attack him.

Forward ear position signals concentration

7 Penetration
Standing astride the female, the male "pedals" with his hindlegs and then makes just a few pelvic thrusts. Mating is over within a few seconds, but he keeps a firm grasp on the nape of her neck to prevent her from turning on him.

8 Withdrawal
The female shrieks as the male withdraws. Hook-like barbs on the male's penis cause genital irritation, thereby stimulating the chain of nervous and hormonal reactions that culminate in ovulation.

Hindlegs pull back

Repeated mating

Mating often occurs as frequently as ten times an hour. It ends only when the male is exhausted, and he may well be replaced by another suitor. A succession of males will await their turn patiently. At the beginning of mating the male makes the advances and is often rebuffed. After repeated matings the female beckons another male with a provocative display. Eggs are released from the ovaries 24 hours after successful matings.

9 Male apprehension *At the moment of her piercing scream the male instantly disengages and moves away. The female will often lash out at the male as soon as he releases her from the neck grasp.*

10 Relaxing together (LEFT) *After mating the female allows the male to sit near her. They will groom themselves in preparation for a subsequent mating.*

Toms and Queens

THERE ARE SEVERAL subtle behavioral differences between male and female cats. Unneutered males are usually more destructive and more active than females. Females are generally more playful and friendly, more inclined to be affectionate and cleaner than their male counterparts.

Male cats roam over large territories, marking them out frequently with their pungent urine. They fight for possession of the territory and for the right to mate with the females within it. Neutering can help to diminish a male cat's need to roam, spray and fight, although it does not always affect all these behaviors to the same extent. Males that are neutered before they reach puberty do not develop secondary sex characteristics, but if they are neutered after puberty all the physical secondary sex characteristics are retained.

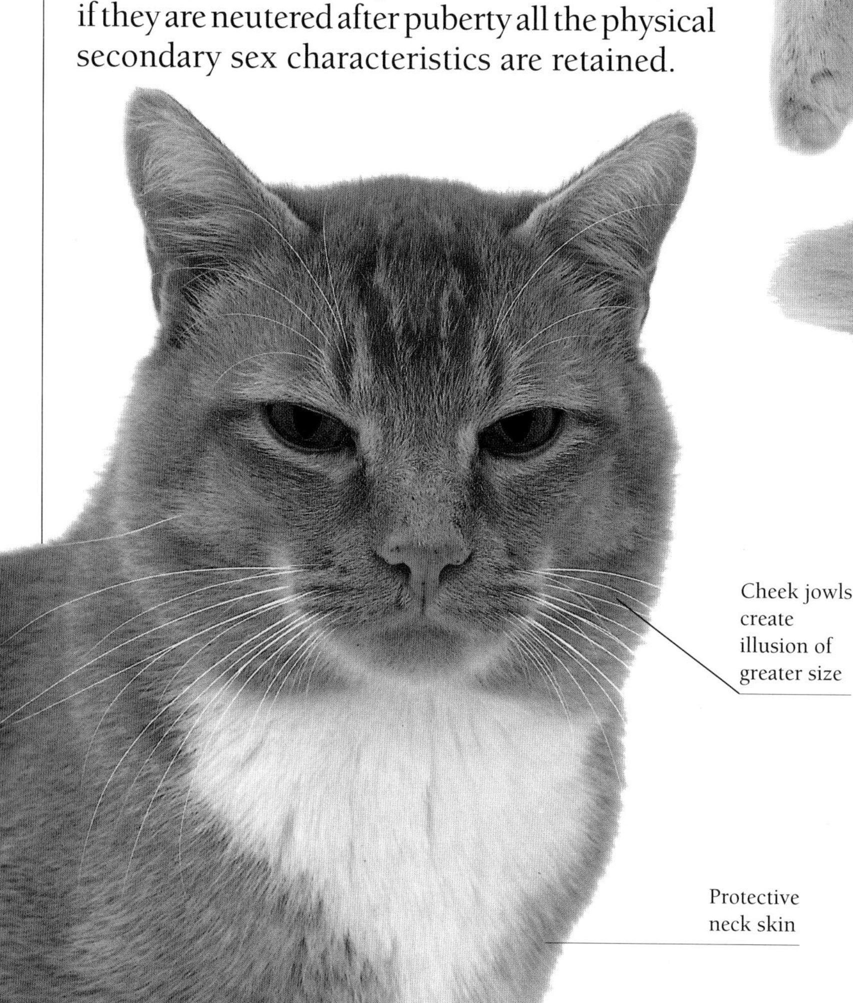

Tomcat
(LEFT) *Secondary sex characteristics – like prominent cheek ruffs and thick neck skin – develop because this tomcat has not been neutered. Likewise, if a lion is neutered before puberty, he will not develop the entire male's mane.*

Entire female
(ABOVE) *This female has a typically delicate face and bone structure. Her slight body is also considerably smaller than a male cat's. In some breeds, females grow to only half the size of their male counterparts.*

Neutered male

(BELOW) Neutering does not seem to have any significant effect on the excitability or destructiveness of male cats. If males develop unpleasant sex-related behaviors, neutering after the behavior develops is just as effective in correcting it as neutering before the problem arises.

Neutered female

(ABOVE) Neutering has a far less dramatic effect on female behavior than on male. Males and females have significantly different behavior repertoires from each other, but once neutered their behaviors tend to be more similar to the unneutered female than the unneutered male. Neutering reduces the need to roam, so all neutered cats are more likely to stay closer to the home territory of your yard.

Effects of neutering

When a male cat reaches puberty, the male hormone goes into constant production. Secondary sex characteristics then begin to develop. These characteristics include pungent urine odor for territory marking and behaviors such as sex-related aggression. Females, however, display sex-related behavioral changes only when they are in season since this is when high levels of the sex hormone are produced. So while neutering dramatically suppresses male behavior, the neutered female cat simply behaves like a constantly out-of-season female cat.

Getting Older

As YOUR CAT ages, you may notice that his mood changes. Some cats become grumpy and irritable, while others grow more affectionate, seeking out their owner for comfort. Old age can also bring on a change in your cat's appetite – he may develop preferences for certain foods, or demand to be fed more or less frequently.

Hearing deteriorates

Matted coat develops as he finds grooming difficult

Reacting slowly

In old age, nerve messages take longer to arrive at and to be sent from the brain. Sometimes the first messages to arrive can temporarily block the entire system. As a result, the brain appears to be working in slow motion, and your cat may not react as quickly as he did when he was younger. This means accidents are more likely. There is also a tendency for your cat to respond in a way that is unfamiliar to you, behaving more like a feral cat. He may even lash out at you when you stroke him. If this happens, it is not because you have provoked him – he has simply forgotten his "learned" behavior and is reverting to natural instincts.

Aging gracefully

The gradual changes of old age are inevitable, but your elderly pet will give you just as much pleasure in his later years as he did when he was a kitten. You may need to change the way you treat your cat when he gets past his prime. For example, try not to disturb him unnecessarily when he is sleeping. Let him decide when he wants to be stroked. Reduce the amount of protein in his diet, since he will need less energy and his kidneys are not as efficient. A well-cared for pet cat should live to be 15 years or older.

Putting on weight

(LEFT) *This Persian has put on a few extra pounds in his old age. His coat has also developed matts because he finds it difficult to groom. It is unusual for a healthy cat to become overweight. Unlike dogs, they are not obsessive about food – although some are accidentally trained by their owners to be so.*

Losing weight

(RIGHT) *In her advancing years this cat has grown to be rather thin. Overactivity of the thyroid gland sometimes causes cats to become hyperactive, which can result in dramatic weight loss.*

"I've got to take it easy – I'm not the cat I used to be."

Eyesight begins to fail

Prominent shoulder blade indicates gradual weight loss

Coat becomes patchy in places

TAMING OF THE CAT

THERE ARE FEW differences between the pet cat lying by an open fire and its relative, the North African wild cat. They both have the same fundamental repertoire of cat behavior, but to differing degrees.

It is only in the last 100 years that we have seriously interfered in cat breeding. In previous centuries, by selecting certain cats to accompany them on voyages around the world, our forebears unknowingly helped to create breeds or regional differences. For example, cats with too many toes are common in the northeastern United States because some of the first cats taken there by British settlers had that genetic trait and bred with each other. Through selective breeding, we are now creating breeds not only for their different appearances, but also

Blotched effect
The blotched tabby pattern has become dominant in many parts of the world. The highest concentration is still in Britain.

Rarity value
The Persian's long coat is the result of a genetic accident that has been perpetuated because we admire it.

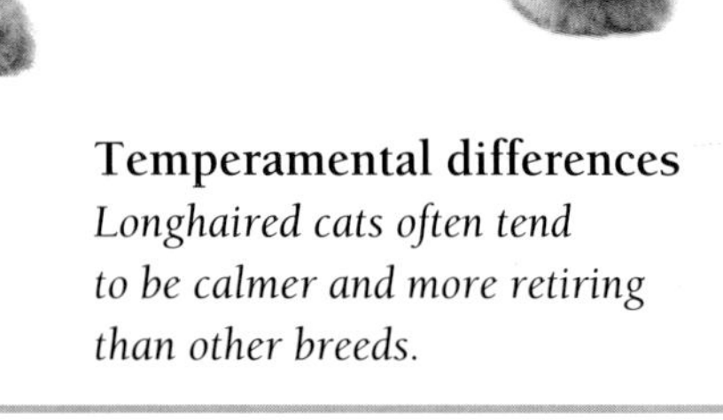

Temperamental differences
Longhaired cats often tend to be calmer and more retiring than other breeds.

Behavior patterns
Compact, chunky cats like this tom are common in Europe. In North America, similar cats are longer, leaner and more outgoing.

for the resulting variety of cat personalities. Longhaired Persian cats evolved in eastern Turkey, Iraq and Iran but are now selectively bred worldwide. They are quieter and less demonstrative than most shorthaired felines. At the opposite end of the spectrum, the increasingly popular Burmese was restricted to a small area of Southeast Asia until less than 50 years ago. Today, these effusive, gregarious, vocal cats are popular throughout all of Europe, Australasia and the Americas.

Gender differences
This unneutered female is less aggressive, cleaner and friendlier to humans than an unneutered male would be.

New breeds such as the gentle Ragdolls and Burmillas and the more assertive Devon Rexes are also becoming increasingly popular. Your cat's breeding history is a significant factor in determining its personality, so it is wise to bear this in mind when choosing a cat to fit into your home environment.

New breeds
Originally existing in small numbers in Burma and Thailand, the Burmese has achieved worldwide popularity in the last 30 years.

Your Pet's Ancestors

YOUR PET CAT, a descendant of the North African wild cat, retains instincts and behaviors similar to his wild cousins. The wild cat is highly adaptable, capable of responding to novel situations and shows little fear of humans. In fact, its natural behavioral makeup includes an ability to live in close proximity to man. Thousands of years ago, the wild cat chose of its own accord to become domesticated, willingly relinquishing the life of the lone hunter.

Instinctive hunter
(ABOVE) Even as the North African wild cat evolved into a domestic animal, it retained the ability to be self-sufficient. The Norwegian forest cat, a descendant of the tamed African wild cat, reverted to the wild where it survived as a superb hunter. Because its ancestors had contact with man it has a more relaxed temperament than wild cats indigenous to northern Africa, which have never been domesticated.

Living close to man
(RIGHT) Forebear of today's domestic cat, the North African wild cat is drawn to human settlements where it can scavenge for a meal.

Surviving alone (ABOVE) *Timid and reclusive, the European wild cat does not have the genetic potential to alter its behavior, and has not been able to adapt to living with man. Impossible to tame, this cat has had little part in the evolution of the pet cat.*

Growing a longer coat

The shorthaired coat of the North African wild cat consists of two types of hair – short, fine down hairs and longer, thicker guard hairs. Most longhaired cats evolved as the result of a genetic mutation that allowed the down hair to continue to grow. The long down hairs tangle easily. The longhaired Norwegian forest cat and the Maine Coon have longer guard hairs, which do not get matted, so these cats are able to survive without help from us with grooming.

Maine Coon
A descendant of the hardy American farm cat, the Maine Coon has a luxurious coat to cope with a harsh climate. Thanks to their large size, the cats can catch rabbits, a widely available prey.

Becoming Domesticated

CHOOSING TO LIVE near human settlements, the North African wild cat gradually shifted from hunting for his food in the wild to scavenging. Villages provided a source of food, and the cat's diet was supplemented with the mice and rats that infested grain stores. Inevitably, some of the cats, perhaps the most gentle ones and probably those that begged for food, were adopted as pets. Domestication and selective breeding had begun. Enjoying the considerable benefits of human companionship, the wild cat willingly became tame.

Reacting with fear
(LEFT) *This wild kitten reacts viciously toward his handler because he is unused to this kind of contact and has not been socialized by human companionship.*

Scavenging successfully
(ABOVE) *Today, the North African wild cat is sometimes seen close to human habitation in parts of the Sudan. The villagers take no domestic interest in them, but the cats show little fear as they scavenge from the wastes of the community.*

Silent survivor
Until recently, cats were reviled in the Singapore peninsula. The immigrant cats therefore evolved into small and silent scavengers rather than ardent beggars.

Adapting to circumstance
There are no obvious physical differences between wild and domestic cats, but the latter has developed a longer intestinal tract to cope with a more varied diet. Domestic cats can also develop unusual tastes if encouraged to do so.

Mutual benefits

Your pet cat is a beggar and expects you to provide regular meals. He no longer needs to be a good hunter to survive. It is natural for you to enjoy the fact that your cat depends on you for the necessities of life. The reliance behavior is being perpetuated through intervention in breeding, and, in time, the ability of cats to hunt successfully will diminish, and an exaggerated dependence on humans will develop.

Begging effectively
This kitten learned at an early age to demand milk from her mother. This behavior is perpetuated in the adult mother cat as she meows and reaches up to beg food from her owner. Mimicking her mother, the kitten quickly learns how to survive.

Defining Characteristics

THE DESCENDANTS OF the North African wild cat were first cherished as domestic pets in their native land in about 1000 BC. Merchants then discovered that cats were good traveling companions because they could decimate their ships' rat populations. They were also valuable commodities, fetching high prices in foreign parts. As the merchants sailed the trade routes, so cats spread around the world. Breeding was, of course, restricted to other cats within the same imported group, so the physical and temperamental characteristics that merchants had originally selected were perpetuated.

Above 80%
70-80%
60-70%
50-60%
40-50%
30-40%
20-30%
Above 10%

Blotched tabby
(RIGHT) This blotched tabby pattern is uncommon in northern Africa. Traders sought out the cats with the most unusual coats to take with them on their ships.

Blotched tabby trail
(ABOVE) The blotched or classic tabby pattern occurs in less than 20 percent of the cats living in northern Africa. The incidence of this pattern increases as the old trade routes are followed through Europe, reaching up to as much as 80 percent in some areas of Britain, the end of the old trade routes.

Striped tabby
(LEFT) The striped tabby is now rare, although it was the original pattern of the northern African domesticated cat. Today, most striped tabbies have some blotched pattern as well.

Tame colors

Merchants often singled out cats with blue, chocolate and other nonagouti coats to take with them on their journeys. (A nonagouti coat is made up of hairs that are uniform in color from root to tip.) Cats possessing these coat colors were possibly less intimidated by humans and also less aggressive. The cats interbred in their new environments, so the resulting cat population tended to have gentler, tamer personalities.

Black magic

(ABOVE) *This black cat typifies nonagouti coat color. Black cats were initially admired for their looks, but in Europe they became associated with worship of the devil. Even today many superstitions exist.*

Following trade routes

The North African wild cat has the genetic potential to produce descendants with a great variety of fur colors, such as this blue and orange coat. The further the distance traveled on the trade routes from northern Africa, the greater the incidence of unusual colors.

Too many toes

All breeds of cats can produce kittens with extra toes on their front paws. These are known as polydactyls. In general, there are fewer than 10 percent polydactyls in any cat population. However, many of the very first cats to arrive in North America in the region from Boston, Massachusetts, to Halifax, Nova Scotia, carried with them the genetic potential for extra toes. A limited availability of breeding partners resulted in a higher than average percentage of polydactyls in the cat population of that region.

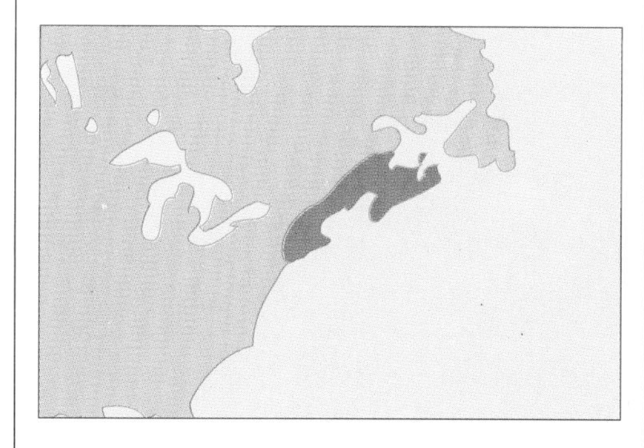

Restricted population

A high incidence of polydactyls occurs along the east coast of North America.

Harmless deformity

Instead of the normal five toes, polydactyl cats often have seven toes on their forepaws.

Adapting to Habitats

As long as 3000 years ago, cats began colonizing the world. The first were taken by merchants from northern Africa to Europe and Asia. Traders also took cats to China via Babylon and India. Cats were initially introduced to Japan around AD 1000, although it was another 500 years before they reached the Americas. The only cats to survive were those able to cope with the demands of a new environment.

Small beginnings
(BELOW) *Four thousand years ago, the domestic cat inhabited only a small area of northern Africa.*

Worldwide distribution
(RIGHT) *Today cats have colonized almost the entire world, except for the cold Arctic and Antarctic regions.*

Hardy survivor
The large-sized Maine Coon breed developed from the hardy farm cat, originally taken to the United States of America by early British immigrants. Living off a diet of rabbits, the cats flourished. To survive the harsh winters in New England, they evolved thick but trouble-free coats.

Survival of the fittest

The first cats to be introduced to a region could, of course, only mate with other new arrivals. Interbreeding then led to populations with a restricted genetic pool, threatening the health of future generations. Only the fittest survived, and the first breeds began to evolve. Adapting to Thailand's heat, for example, the cat's coat thinned out, while in the mountainous Van district of Turkey, cats developed thicker coats.

Easy-care coat
(RIGHT) *Short hair, which is far easier to manage than long hair, is the most common type of coat in domestic cats in Europe. The British Shorthair has sturdy, short legs and a muscular body. There is a wide range of colors and coat patterns.*

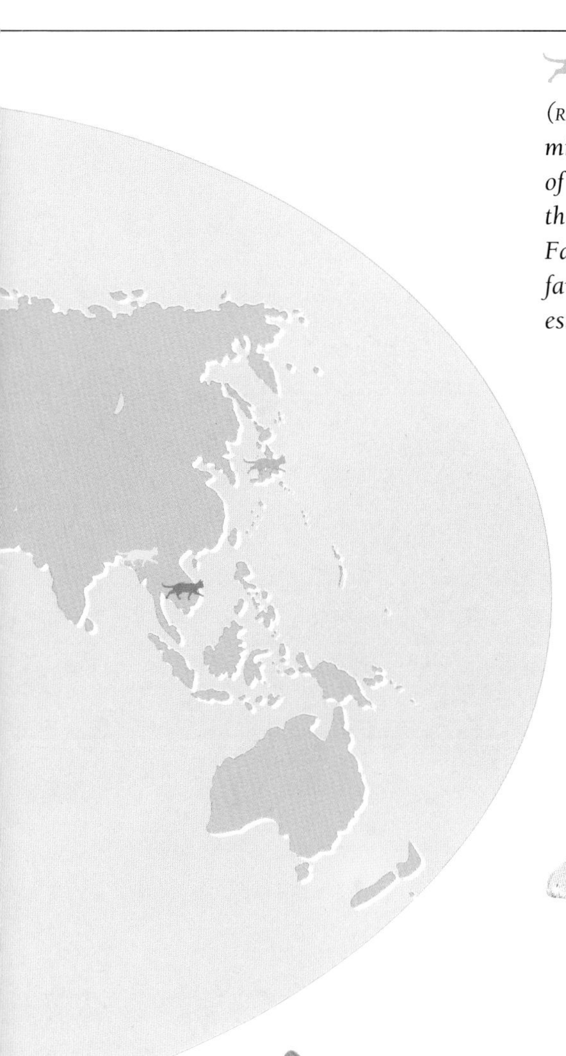

Powder-puff tail

(RIGHT) *The result of a genetic mistake, the short, curly, fluffy tail of the Japanese Bobtail survived in the closed breeding population of the Far East. The breed is a firm family favorite in Japan, where it has been established for hundreds of years.*

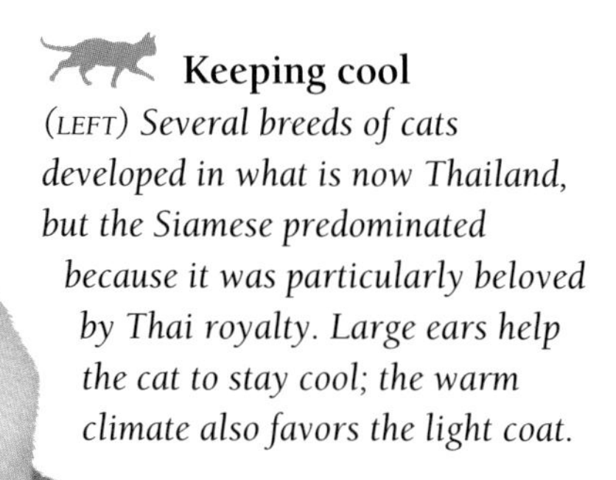

Keeping cool

(LEFT) *Several breeds of cats developed in what is now Thailand, but the Siamese predominated because it was particularly beloved by Thai royalty. Large ears help the cat to stay cool; the warm climate also favors the light coat.*

Exotic looks

(BELOW) *Longhaired cats originated in Asia Minor. It is thought that the long coat evolved as a result of a genetic change in only a few cats. These cats survived, and so in future interbreeding the long hair was perpetuated. Today, longhaired breeds rely on humans for their survival since they need help with grooming.*

Water-loving cat

This breed evolved naturally in the isolated region around Lake Van in Turkey. The long, silky coat molts during the hot Turkish summer.

Newcomer

(ABOVE) *This is a popular new breed and is the result of a cross between a brown female imported from Burma to the United States in the 1930s and a Siamese tom.*

Personality Traits

Cat personality and coat color are probably genetically linked. By developing preferences for cats with certain coat colors and lengths, and specific eye colors, we have created breeds of cats that are distinctive from each other. Although the cats were selected for their appearance, individual breeds also seem to have evolved different personalities. Siamese cats are energetic and vociferous, while longhaired cats tend to be more placid. Oriental shorthairs are extroverts, but intolerant of other cats.

Friendly colors
(ABOVE) Although it has been suggested that nontabby cats are friendlier than tabbies, there is no firm evidence to indicate significant behavior differences between them.

Ornamental Persians
(ABOVE) Longhaired cats may look cuddly, but they are not as affectionate as some other breeds, although they are friendly toward other household cats.

High-strung types
(BELOW) Both Siamese and Burmese breeds are excitable. Siamese may also be unfriendly to other felines in your house. Cats are not usually destructive, but these breeds are the most likely to cause mayhem in the home.

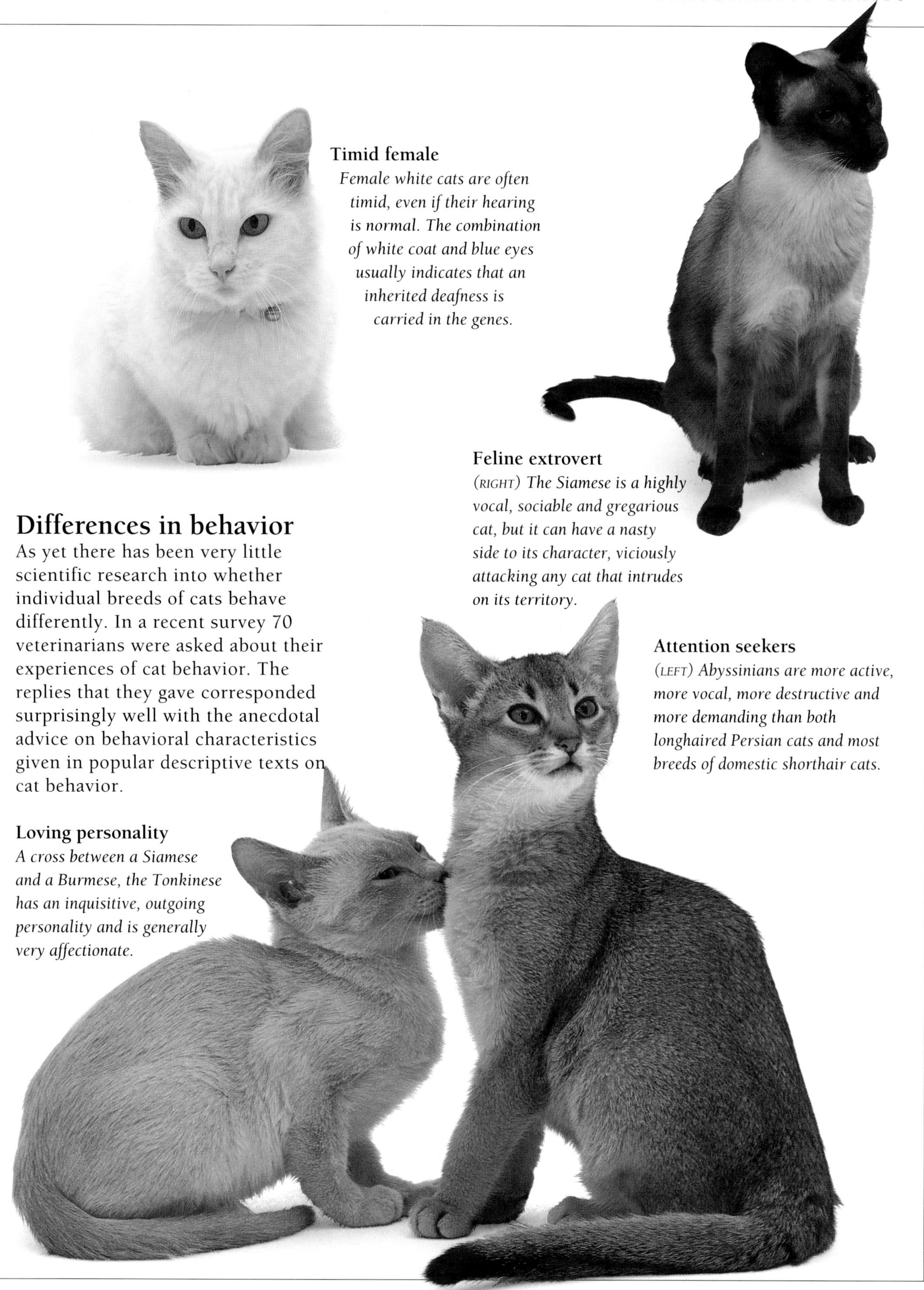

Timid female
Female white cats are often timid, even if their hearing is normal. The combination of white coat and blue eyes usually indicates that an inherited deafness is carried in the genes.

Feline extrovert
(RIGHT) *The Siamese is a highly vocal, sociable and gregarious cat, but it can have a nasty side to its character, viciously attacking any cat that intrudes on its territory.*

Differences in behavior

As yet there has been very little scientific research into whether individual breeds of cats behave differently. In a recent survey 70 veterinarians were asked about their experiences of cat behavior. The replies that they gave corresponded surprisingly well with the anecdotal advice on behavioral characteristics given in popular descriptive texts on cat behavior.

Attention seekers
(LEFT) *Abyssinians are more active, more vocal, more destructive and more demanding than both longhaired Persian cats and most breeds of domestic shorthair cats.*

Loving personality
A cross between a Siamese and a Burmese, the Tonkinese has an inquisitive, outgoing personality and is generally very affectionate.

Analyzing Cat Character

CAT OWNERS INTUITIVELY understand that each cat is an individual with its own personality. Defining the individual's uniqueness is difficult. All cats share their behaviors with all other cats, but it is the varying degrees of these behaviors that create temperaments.

Each individual is affected by genetics, hormones, the environment in which the cat finds itself and by learning. This means that some breeds almost certainly have traits that can be described as "breed personality." The Siamese, for example, is more vocal than other breeds. Research with other mammals, such as foxes and rats, has shown that personality is linked to coat color. To date, however, no large surveys have been conducted to find whether personality is associated with breed of cat.

Cat images

Everyone has his or her own perception of cats. Many associate felines with warmth, sensuousness, softness and all things maternal and feminine. Judging from their uses in advertising, this is an increasingly common perception, which is good for cats because it is more likely that we will care for them generously.

Unfortunately, some people – almost one in four – think cats are cunning, spiteful and deceitful, and so they treat them with disdain.

Shy personality
(LEFT) This long-haired tortoiseshell has a more withdrawn personality and is quieter than the average cat.

Oriental build
Cats with long, lean bodies are more likely to have gregarious, outgoing personalities than their sturdier cousins. They are also more protective of their home territories and are usually more vocal and demonstrative.

Your cat's personality

Cat owners tend to be good observers. Asking owners about their cat's behavior is one way scientists can research cat personality. You can assess your cat using the questionnaire below. Score each group of questions separately to find out how alert, sociable and equable your cat is.

To analyze your cat's personality, complete this simple questionnaire by checking the appropriate box. If you would like to help in a worldwide study, please photocopy the completed questionnaire and send it to: Bruce Fogle, DVM, Box DK, 86 York Street, London W1H IDP, England.

Assess the behavior of your cat by checking the appropriate box.	Almost always (1)	Usually (2)	Sometimes (3)	Rarely (4)	Almost never (5)
MY CAT:					
Tolerates handling					
Is affectionate					
Demands attention					
Is confident					
Accepts strangers					
MY CAT IS:					
Excitable					
Vocal					
Playful					
Active					
Destructive					
Independent					
MY CAT IS:					
Fearful of familiar cats					
Hostile to strange cats					
Solitary					
Aggressive					
Tense					

Sociable

A low score (12 or less) means your cat is highly sociable and well integrated in human society. Cats that have matured before they meet humans are poorly socialized and likely to have high scores.

Alert

Cats with low scores are the most lively and alert. These felines often have energy to burn and may need organized activity; otherwise they become destructive. A high score (over 15) indicates a reserved or listless pet.

Equable

Cats that enjoy cat company will score high (over 12) and usually include cats raised from kittenhood with other cats. A low score indicates a cat hater, either too territorial to allow another cat on its turf, or too set in its ways to change its attitude.

- How old was your cat when you acquired him/her?__________
- How old is your cat now?__________
- Is your cat male or female?__________ ☐ M ☐ F
- Has your cat been neutered?__________ ☐ Yes ☐ No
- Does your cat have free access to the outdoors?__________ ☐ Yes ☐ No
- In what country do you live?__________
- What is the breed of your cat?__________
- What color is your cat? __________

USEFUL ADDRESSES

American Cat Association

8101 Katherine Ave.
Panorama City, CA 91402
(818) 782-6080

American Cat Fanciers' Association, Inc.

Highway 248
Branson, MO 65616
(417) 334-5430

American Society for the Prevention of Cruelty to Animals

441 East 92 St.
New York, NY 10128
(212) 876-7700

Canadian Cat Association

83 Kennedy Road South,
Unit 1805
Brampton, Ontario,
Canada L6W 3P3
(416) 459-1481

The Cat Fanciers' Association, Inc.

1805 Atlantic Ave.
Manasquan, NJ 08736
(908) 528-9797

Cat Fanciers' Federation

9509 Montgomery Road
Cincinnati, OH 45242
(513) 984-1841

The Cat Fanciers' Newsletter

304 Hastings St.
Redlands, CA 92373
(714) 793-5061

Cat Fancy

P.O. Box 6050
Mission Viejo, CA 92690
(714) 855-8822

Cats Magazine

P.O. Box 290037
Port Orange, FL 32129
(904) 788-2770

Cat World International

P.O. Box 35635
Phoenix, AZ 85069
(602) 995-1822

I Love Cats

950 Third Ave., 16th Floor
New York, NY 10022
(212) 888-1855

The International Cat Association

P.O. Box 2684
Harlingen, TX 78551
(512) 428-8046

INDEX

ACKNOWLEDGMENTS

Author's acknowledgments

Almost all of my professional hours are spent in clinical practice but when I need a little writing time Jenny Berry and Amanda Topp, two exceptionally good veterinary nurses, hold the fort. Many thanks. The same applies to my family, especially my wife Julia, who lets me disappear into the country each weekend to concentrate on writing.

I did not know it at the time, and I am sure that he did not realize it either, but my father, through his collection of animals, primed me from childhood to have an interest in animal behavior. As I write this he remains a healthy octogenarian, proud as Punch of what his youngest son does. I hope he enjoys showing this book to his friends.

Dorling Kindersley would like to thank:

For book design and illustration Cooper·Wilson; for computer graphics Salvo Tomasselli; for editorial assistance Corinne Hall, Charyn Jones, Stephanie Jackson, Jackie Douglas and Vicky Davenport; for the index Karin Woodruff; for design assistance Juliet Cooke; for picture research Diana Morris; for providing cats for photography on location Natasha Guttmann, Esther Bruml, Karen Tanner, Carolyn Stephenson, Blackie Merrifield, Jenny Berry, Jane Burton, Heather Creasey, Liz Button, Lynn Medcalf and Margaret Correia; for location photography Steve Gorton and Tim Ridley; for providing props John Palmer Ltd. (cat brush) and Steetley Minerals Ltd. (cat-litter basket).

Jane Burton would like to thank:

For help to find, handle and feed cats Hazel Taylor, Sue Hall, Di Everet, Les Tolley and Janet Tedder; for lending cats for photography Carolyn Woods; for modelling Arabella Grinstead and Louisa Hall.

Photographic credits

All photography by Jane Burton except for:

Steve Gorton: **p.5** all pics, **p.9** bl, br, **p.11** br, **p.15** tl, bl, **p.16** tc, **p.45** bc, **p.111** bl, **p.117** t, bc, **p.118** c, **p.121** tr.

Tim Ridley: **p.27** bl, **p.34** bl, **pp.40-41** all pics, **p.42** br, **p.46** bl, **p.95** br, **p.107** tr.

Dave King: **p.95** cr, **p.110** br, **p.112** t, **p.120** tr, **p.122** t.

Animals Unlimited: **p.109** br, **p.113** bc, br.

Bruce Coleman Ltd: **p.24** cl, **p.25** tl, **p.110** b, **p.111** tl; *Jane Burton* **p.13** br; *Hans Reinhard* **p.113** t, c.

Marc Henrie: **p.116** c.

David Keith Jones: **p.116** br.

Natural History Photographic Agency: *M. Savonius* **p.86** c.

Key: l = left, r = right, t = top, b = bottom, c = center.

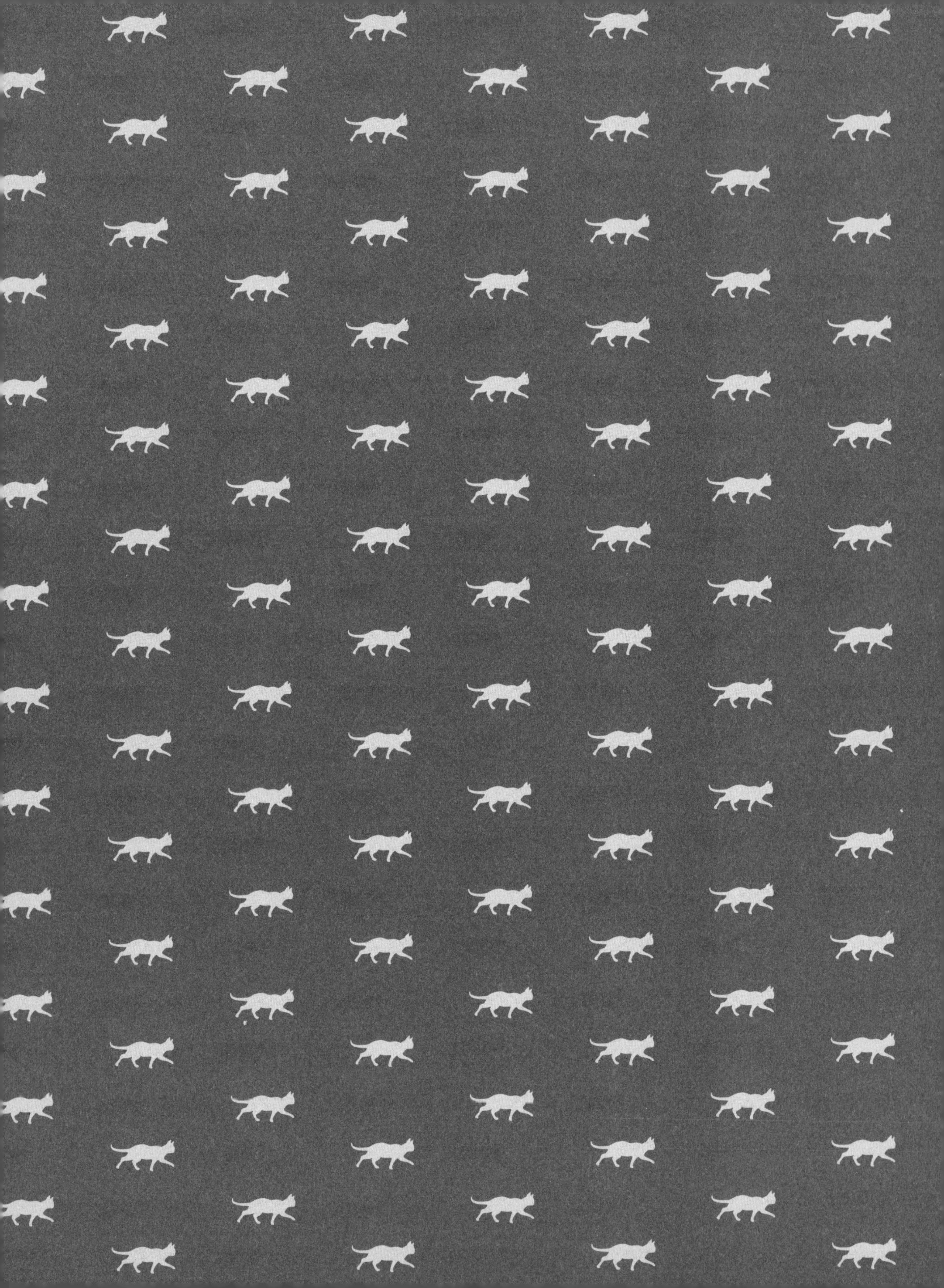